## ACKNOWLEDGEMENTS

My thanks to Abilio Ferreira for encouraging me to write, and sharing his thoughts with the Universe.

# A COSMIC JOURNEY TO THE UNKNOWN

## BY
## Odete Martins Bigote

Copyright © 2019 by Odete Martins Bigote.
All rights reserved
No part of this book may be reproduced, stored in a retrieval system or transmitted by any means, electronic, mechanical, photocopying, recording, or otherwise, without written permission from the author.

ISBN-978-0-578-47801-2

Scripture taken from the New King James Version.
Copyright © 1979,1980,1982 by Thomas Nelson, Inc
Used by permission. All rights reserved.

I am grateful for the acceptance to write, in my own words, about some of the concepts in The Knowledge Book. Copyright © 1996
Published by: Dunya Kardeslik Birligi Mevlana Yuce Vakfi
(World Brotherhood Union Universal Unification Center Association)
P.O.Box 84,34740 Suadiye – ISTANBUL/TURKIYE

The ideas presented herein are the personal interpretation and understanding of the author and are not necessarily endorsed by the copyright holder of the Knowledge Book (World Brotherhood Union Mevlana Supreme Foundation and World Brotherhood Union Universal Unification Center Association)

The purpose of Mrs. Bigote's writings and talks is to educate. Neither the author nor the publisher shall have any liability to anyone with respect to any loss or damage caused by the information contained in her writings and talks.

## DEDICATION

To my angels who have been always with me.

## TABLE OF CONTENTS

Introduction                                                          8

Chapter 1:   The Beginning
             "I know that I am intelligent, because
             I know that I know nothing."
                     Socrates 400BC                                  16

Chapter 2:   The Big Push                                            27

Chapter 3:   How Do We Know
             We Are Progressing?                                     32

Chapter 4:   The Milky Way and the Arts                              37

Chapter 5:   Who is the most famous
             of all provokers?
             Devil, of course                                        47

Chapter 6:   The Ongoing Cycles of Life
             The Thread and The Spool                                53

Chapter 7:   Sex and Love
             Omega's Mission                                         63

Chapter 8:   The Twin Universe
             A Ghost                                                 68

Chapter 9:   "I Think Therefore I am"                                74

Chapter 10:  Where Do Thoughts Come From?                            78

Chapter 11:  Love                                                    83

Chapter 12:  When the Heart Rules                                    86

| | | |
|---|---|---|
| Chapter 13: | Reflections<br>God Created Mankind in<br>His Own Image<br>Why? | 91 |
| Chapter 14: | To Be or Not to Be Normal | 105 |
| Chapter 15: | Where Do Our Geniuses<br>Come From? | 112 |
| Chapter 16: | A Planet of Gold, Music and Color | 117 |
| Chapter 17: | Where is Bertrand Russell? | 121 |
| Chapter 18: | Technology | 123 |
| Chapter 19: | Heaven<br>Rest in Peace | 126 |
| Chapter 20: | Who is the Allah in the<br>Knowledge Book | 136 |
| Chapter 21: | Are Men Fit to Rule Men? | 153 |
| Chapter 22: | A Priori<br>We existed before | 166 |
| Chapter 23: | Prototypes and Reincarnation | 173 |
| Chapter 24: | The Energy Cord/Silver Cord<br>and The Codes | 178 |
| Chapter 25: | Atlanta's Mission | 185 |
| Chapter 26: | Atlanta's Dimension and Allah | 192 |
| Chapter 27: | Why Did Atlanta degenerate? | 198 |
| Chapter 28: | Time Is Illusion | 205 |

| | | |
|---|---|---|
| Chapter 29: | Universes Are One Inside the Other Can We Eliminate Evil? | 210 |
| Chapter 30: | Who Designed our Salvation? | 218 |
| Chapter 31: | Who is Mevlana? | 224 |
| Chapter 32: | Why are Humans Coming Out of the Closet? | 227 |
| Chapter 33: | The Sleeping Giant | 233 |
| Chapter 34: | The Mission on the West | 238 |
| Chapter 35: | Wounded Warrior: Wake up and Cheer | 244 |
| Bibliography | | 254 |
| About the Author | | 255 |

## INTRODUCTION

Why would a Christian, like myself, choose to write a book inspired by a benevolent Allah who works together with Jesus Christ and other well-known Celestial Beings?

As an author, I am always encouraged to write about the need humanity has to be cured and live a harmonious life. Nevertheless, fear associated with words, such as, Love, God, Allah, Creator, death and many others, must be handled in a way that does not hinder our progress.

In principle, words are but symbols, they represent something else. However, the way we interpret words is like the dance of life. They may invoke ideas that distort its true meaning, or they may be free of distortion so that we can see them for what they really are and consider their true values. As an example, due to the present events in history, many of us react to the word Allah in a way that does not represent what he is proposing, and therefore damages his hope for creating sincere human beings, free of evil thoughts. This is manifested by many of us from all backgrounds, especially when we alter information that is beneficial to mankind, without carefully analyzing the content. Then, we base our reports on emotions and superficiality. This is why I recommend the readers to avoid such reports, and not to be discouraged after reading just one or two pages, or sentences of any writings.

Why is this happening? Has humanity ever considered that our major problem is the erroneous thought of separation? This is science, this is spirituality, this is beyond the physical, and this is the truth. But the truth can hurt. The thought of separation prevents us from understanding and accepting what our eyes cannot see, as well as, the influence of Cosmic Energies bathing us 24/7.

It is not natural to be separated. It causes pain and chaos within us and in the world. It blocks mankind from learning how to handle darkness so that we can see The Light. It is obvious that the thought of separation creates fear and plays a major role in our lives.

As a child in Europe, I had an aversion to science. I blamed it all on the teachers. I feared them. Once in New York, I read a book titled One, Two, Three...Infinity. Then, I began to see the connection of all things. The book relieved me of some discomfort about mathematics and science in general. At Columbia University in New York City, I still had problems handling math. I was sent to a private tutor, especially assigned to help students in need. For a few weeks, I was assigned home-work which I enjoyed. One day, the tutor handed it back to me with notes she had written and asked to give them to my teacher. To my great surprise, she congratulated me for my success in such a short time.

Fear was removed. Joy and happiness enveloped me. Books about religion and science are part of life. However, they are not easy to understand and very often they are not taught properly even in schools. The way they are presented can cause fear in some people who are not strong enough to read with an open mind or who come from a different background where their freedoms were curtailed. But this is changing. Why? We are going through three significant Cosmic Ages which consist of powerful waves that serve as the fundamental preparation to purify mankind before a New Golden Age is initiated.

Learning never ends. For that reason, the 20th century was a difficult time for us to endure and the 21st century will also be very challenging. By the 22nd century many of us may start to feel harmony within ourselves, and hopefully are gradually prepared to advance our thought system. It all depends on the progress of each individual's consciousness as a Whole. Some of us will progress. Others, who have chosen to delay their progress, will have to start anew because they have refused guidance which consist of rules and regulations, such as, love and respect for nature and human beings, and the need to take responsibility for our thoughts, as well as actions.

We are constantly going through examinations without being aware.
Who are our teachers? All the invisible, very powerful Celestial Beings from all religions and from no religion. This is the reason why I was inspired by *The Knowledge Book*, (Herein referred to as *The KB* or *The Text*), channeled to Mrs. Vedia Bulent (Onsu) Corak, known as Mevlana, which was introduced to mankind in 1993. It is a book with many characteristics. It emphasizes love, respect and responsibility, so that all of us can become perfect humans.

This great event happened in Turkey, the land of Ataturk, the 1st President of Modern Turkey. His famous slogan was: Peace at home, peace in the world. It is thanks to him that Turkish women are allowed to vote. *The KB* was published by World Brotherhood Union Universal Unification Center Association in Istanbul. I am not affiliated with this Association, and never visited Turkey. As a volunteer, I am an independent author and researcher and do not represent any particular organization. I respect all religions, and people from no religion. *The Text* has 1,085 pages and very often contains complex and dispersed information, on purpose to help us realize the importance of being patient and that learning is interminable.

It is my mission to try and write in the simplest way possible, about some of the concepts that I have learned up to this day. The fact that I consider myself to be on a mission, does not deny that all human beings are on mission.

What follows is a short list of what the reader can expect from reading the Cosmic Journey to The Unknown.

1) The role Atlanta, a mystical state idealized by Plato 350 BC, played in our formation before our existence on earth.
2) We are descendants of the androgynous. They were beings that had the characteristics of both sexes.
3) The importance of DNA, an acid that carries genetic information.
4) The difference from a robot made by men versus a biological robot.
5) Life on a Planet of pure gold.
6) The devil is a learning tool. Our lack of True-Love is what causes chaos.
7) Our form of sexual intercourse is peculiar only to life on earth.
8) In other dimensions children are conceived without physical contact.
9) Our thoughts cause universes to give birth to other universes.
10) As a peaceful Missionary, Allah is the creator Of crude matter, with the help of The Unknown. They work together with Jesus Christ, Moses, Mohammed, Mevlana, and others that we may not be aware. There is no discrimination.
11) Our dream is what caused separation on earth and beyond.
12) Universes are one inside the other, all is entangled.
13) UFOs are trying to disrupt missiles.
14) Our life on earth is nothing new: it is a repetition of things past.

Humanity must conclude that our history is the history of repetition. The reader will find out about many aspect of our lives, past, present and future: before the existence of our planet, before our formation, as well as the reason for our presence on earth and where we are heading.

Reading *The KB* contributes to the development of our consciousness without agitating us. However, no one under the age of 18 is allowed to read it, besides it is also not recommended for people who are troubled. The reader has to be able to function in our world dimension, which is the $3^{rd}$ dimension. He/she has to be able to take responsibilities, since it is here that evolution takes place. Let's appreciate our chance to be on earth at this time in history with a mission assigned to all of us so that we can take the necessary steps to learn to handle our emotions without fear and improve our thought system. Then, we can escape from our present condition, the $3^{rd}$ dimension, and progress to worlds and galaxies where they have more advanced technology and know how to handle their thoughts differently.

But, in some galaxies, their inhabitants have no idea of the existence of love, soul and consciousness, at least the way we see them. This is why our mission on earth is very important, so that we unify our consciousness and reflect to The Beyond. Who, in accordance with the information given to Mevlana, has been in charge of implementing in a harmonious way, a method that leads humanity to become perfect human beings? Allah is.

Still, as it is written in *The* KB, he is not alone. He works together with many other Powers. All of them are messengers of *The Unknown*, and work in unison to help us achieve unification without the use of force. The fact that they have always worked in unison corroborates the affirmation that all things are unified, even universes: This is science. This is the truth. This concept that I've learned in my spiritual quest for many decades, has caused a great effect in my life. Indeed, our mission is beyond frontiers: we need to unify our consciousness, on earth and beyond. Of course, in our world, it is easier for us to see separation everywhere. But, deep down in our hearts, we know that we share a "particle" that unites all there is.

If you think there are too many spies on earth, you will be surprised to find out that all of us, human beings, are watched 24/7 and taped by those Beings beyond space and time who are our monitors, our teachers. We are never alone. Many of them are very Powerful Beings that we already know, while others, we never heard of them. Like us, they are on a mission. They guide us, they watch us, they tape our thoughts in what we may consider to be some kind of very advanced form of computers unknown to us on earth. The truth about our computers is that they are nothing but copies that the Celestial Beings allow our technologists to receive in accordance with our development. That is why technology, on earth, is advancing at a great speed, as everybody notices. The more mankind's thought system progresses as a Whole, meaning all of us, the more advanced information we get from beyond space and time in all aspects of our lives. We can see the proof of what is written as we look around at our world. This is why I appreciate the truthfulness described by The Celestial Beings, and have chosen to write about it. It has been a great challenge for me.

Although I never read the Koran, I have read and studied the Christian Bible, along with other spiritual, scientific and philosophical books, such as, A Course in Miracles, Life and Teaching of the Masters of the Far East, Plato, Albert Einstein and

Stephen Hawking. In spite of the fact that I was not born in America, I graduated from New York University, and Columbia University. I devoted decades to reading, writing, lecturing and producing my own cable TV show. I have written books on the topic of spirituality and metaphysics, as well as many articles published on my website. As a matter of fact, some of the concepts described in my previous books, are repeated in The Cosmic Journey to the Unknown. The reason is that, "There is nothing new under the sun." As I kept repeating the same concepts that I researched and wrote about more than 20 years ago, I realized that our history is the history of repetition. Finally, the time came when I became aware of how tired I was of rerunning the same "movie," over and over again and mention that we are not separate. The reality is that we exist as a Whole, that is, all of us are unified, not in a physical form but as consciousness. Yet we are going through a temporary dream of separation.

Therefore, while we are on this planet, separation is an illusion that keeps us sleeping, just like Adam. Our need to awaken is evident, as described in most spiritual and some non-spiritual writings. When I promised myself that I would not get involved with any more books and got rid of many if my possessions, I came across *The Knowledge Book* by chance; it fell on my lap. Later on, I realized that it was not by chance, but an invitation for me to choose to buy it and read it. I was intrigued by the energy, the concepts, and the information presented, most of which I did not understand during my first readings and some I still do not understand after eight years.

Often, we forget what we read. It is wiped out from our memory, usually because we are not ready to receive and act upon the information. In order to help us remember, repetition is necessary. Until, one day, much to our surprise, we may recall everything when our guides realize that we are ready. This does not mean that they control us. What it means is that we are free to choose when to advance in our spiritual development. In spite of these events, I have chosen to devote years to reading, studying and eventually writing. Then, I realized that our reaction has to do with the energy implanted in the letters of *The Text* by a technique peculiar only to *The KB,* based on Light at a speed that cannot be measured on earth. Its ultimate source is always the Divine, described in *The Text* as *The Unknown.*

*The Knowledge Book* is not a religious and or a political book, yet it contains details pertaining to many aspects of life. It is not an indoctrination into any belief. However, we must believe in our ourselves, we must have confidence that we can learn to live a harmonious life while we are on this planet, and even beyond. *The KB* is a complement to all societies. It is a healing book, a guide that leads mankind to better worlds. Together with other books I've studied and applied, it plays a major role in my own healing process. I know it will help humanity. This is why I wrote A Cosmic Journey to *The Unknown*.

Odete Martins Bigote, January 2019

# CHAPTER 1
## THE BEGINNING
## "I KNOW THAT I AM INTELLIGENT, BECAUSE I KNOW THAT I KNOW NOTHING."
### SOCRATES, 400BC

Humanity's only problem is the thought of separation, which is very important for us to consider while on earth. We believe that our thoughts are limited to our planet earth only, and try and ignore The Beyond; this is the cause of our pains.

We have heard and read about a huge explosion that happened before the world began, in an interval beyond space and time. It became known as the Big Bang. Recently, thanks to our advances specially in technology, we have been able to explore the importance of this great event that brought light to darkness. The Big Bang has become a model by which scientists attempt to explain the origin of the universe. Others prefer to see it as an immense Atom that exploded and brought all knowledge to the universe, while at the same time created the illusion of separation, with many galaxies and many worlds. It is our mission to return to that immense Atom.

The good news is that we do not have to be scientists to accept or even understand its implications. We have been taught that Light is the source of all there is. It is in everything and everywhere, and certainly within us. The truth about light is that we do not really see it. What we see are its reflections and the ramifications of this will be explored in a later chapter. Only a few of us are aware that Light conveys information to all there is, especially to genes which are inside the cells. Cells create themselves and they are God's consciousness.

Therefore, it should be no surprise to realize that information comes from Light and is knowledge: It leads to awareness and consciousness. Then, we begin to be aware of the fact that there is no separation and one event leads to another and to another. Without knowledge there can be no consciousness and vice versa. Information came from beyond space and time through the Big Bang and then from DNA before any form existed, including Adam and Eve. As we know, DNA is an acid that carries genetic information and is very important for us to understand life on this planet.

Then, in accordance with our development, we received our powers from the Unknown. This *event* demonstrates that all of us are reflections mentioned coming from the Unknown, which have been with us since before the beginning of time. Their aim is to help all cosmoses, that is, all worlds not just ours, peacefully unify their consciousness. This is a reminder that independent of what galaxy, planet, dimension we are in, thoughts exist and our consciousness must be unified as a Whole. Unification starts with each individual, then it reflects to all there is on this planet and beyond.

Let's bear in mind the famous sentence by the French philosopher Descartes, "I think, therefore I Am." He realized that he exists because he can think and therefore he is conscious of his existence. As we have read, information is supplied by the Light.
But the sentence can also be written differently,
"I Am, therefore I think."
Why?

Because to think we have to be conscious and have knowledge. If I am aware of this then, I can conclude that I exist.

Now, an important question arises; which one came first, consciousness or thought? This question may be clarified by the concept that all things are one inside the other, meaning that they are unified, including universes. Consciousness being light and knowledge is thought and cannot be detached. Herein lies the confirmation that there is no separation. The effect of this sentence is enormous: it involves consciousness, it involves Wholeness, it involves love, it involves all there is. It is our mission while on earth to be aware of this truth. Now we learn again where pain comes from. It comes from the thought of separation which is not real because it sets all there is apart. In other words, as we know, it is not natural to be separated.

Reflect on this. Before the Big Bang and therefore crude matter, consciousness was unified as a Whole until we started to dream of a split. This dream happened long before our existence on earth in a dimension known as Atlanta which will be described in later chapters. Our mission while on earth is to go back to that state of Wholeness. Although each individual is responsible for this return, we can unify only as a *Whole*, not individually. This is the reason why it seems to take so long for us to unify. This is why humans need the sincere cooperation of humans. Of course, this great task is being achieved by each of us through our reflections that lead to the masses. What this means is that our thoughts extend to the infinite and are received by those individuals who are ready to assimilate them, independent of the distance that separates us.

For some people life on earth is an entertainment. We choose to play games, without realizing that we project our problems on others, including on The Unknown. It is about time that we get ready to change our minds and work on ourselves.

For many centuries we have been aware of helpers, such as Buddha, The Masters of The Far East, Moses, Jesus, Mohammed, and others. These Beings have been criticized, abused, and their teachings too often mishandled by human beings, including religious leaders. The conclusion is that even religion has not helped mankind to successfully realize complete unification.

But now what is described as the 4th Plan, which started in the year 2,000, enters the picture. And in all truthfulness, we are informed about where we are heading. We are told that in order to achieve salvation, we must first learn to handle our thoughts differently and in a peaceful way.

We learn in school that DNA is made up of acids that exist in our genes and environment. It is within the cells of all living things, regardless of species. One of the tasks of the genes is to prepare the codes to be stored in the cells. These codes pertain to the inherited history of all living things. Their mission is to impart and manifest the knowledge from very powerful sources that has been accumulated since the beginning of time. This makes it easier to study life on earth, as well as our development, which can seem painfully slow. In addition, DNA contains proteins and amino acids essential to our existence. They also carry billions of centuries of detailed information about our parents, the environment, and our many lives on earth. All events are connected in an endless movement. This means that Light travels to the earth, and then from earth back to the beyond, carrying the information it has gleaned from us. Not a single thought or feeling is lost. Light imparts the information we need in order to progress, but it also receives our reaction and takes it back to our Source.

    We know that genes are inside the cells.

    What about the nucleus which is also inside the cells? We have been taught that every piece of matter, even the tiniest ones, contains a mass with an energy beyond words, known as the nucleus. This is what forms the center of the Atom and therefore, our nucleic world. This also means that ours is a world with countless nuclei, but its origin is One Nucleus only. The nucleus was also manifested on earth through the Big Bang. Its function is to transfer genetic information from parents to offspring, while the function of the genes is to prepare codes. But it is also through the nucleus and genes that reproduction happens on earth, leading to the fact that we are biological robots.

Don't be disturbed by this concept.

Why? We were created not by men but by the Divine: It is the Divine that guides us without interfering and helps mankind to handle all the knowledge within. For now, let's ponder: How many people do we know that try to make a baby for years without succeeding? Until, one day it happens, or it may never happen. The reason is because it is not we, in human form, that choose what has already been chosen before we came to earth.

There has to be a coordination organized and structured beyond our comprehension. For that reason, the importance of our formation as fetus must be respected, and the Power of the Invisible must be accepted, whether we believe in a God or not. We have the proof of what happens to some women who survive abortion: we have seen them in the news; They are beautiful people, and are grateful for their existence. For that reason, we must realized that we are biological robots. We are not robots created by men, and implanted with information as per ego's wishes.

Again, let's recall that we are created by Love. It is Love that implants all the information in us, and always guides us. To recap, inside each cell, we have a nucleus that transfers information; then we have genes, the function of which is to prepare codes. Our consciousness is integral in the relationship between cell evolution and genes. This enormous task is accomplished by Mohammed and Jesus Christ, so it is written. Whether we like it or not, it is important to remember again and again that all Celestial Beings work in corporation with each other and that there is no separation.

All things are one inside the other: this is the core of life. Although all Powers have different names attributed to them, names are nothing but symbols, the purpose of which is to call our attention to the fact that they are an image, a representation of something or someone else. For instance, Allah is a symbol of the Unknown.

In addition, one aim of coding is to register our emotions, especially when the ego is inflated by the information we receive and harbor. Then, in accordance with our needs, Celestial Beings, beyond space and time, can adjust the cosmic influences they send us. All of us, whether we believe it or not, are invited to watch how we handle our thoughts. In other words, we are always being watched and all is registered in what may be regarded as computers beyond the earth. This is a method that has been set up and cannot be changed. The question is: Is our consciousness, that is, our information and knowledge advancing towards unification, or are we going back to the Middle Ages?

Let's be aware that in order to have codes, it is necessary first of all to have knowledge that organizes and structures all lives. This means that DNA had to be created by a Powerful Intelligence from beyond the earth, beyond words and comprehension.

Take a moment and ask yourself: How is it possible for the universe to be

so well organized, in spite of its chaotic and controversial beginnings? We are aware that science is speculative; it is guessing and making suppositions which leads us to ponder. It is also theory, and changes to keep up with our slow development. All events are programmed to suit our needs.
They are blessings from Superior Beings. In other words, the more we progress as a Whole, the more detailed information we receive. This is why events are planned to give us "pushes," which are incentives towards our development and may even be considered provocations.

In the end, the conclusion is that I, like Socrates and everyone else, know that what we know comes from the Unknown; in other words, we are aware that by ourselves we know nothing, because what we know is what we are taught by The Invisible Powers. Yet, we choose to ignore the Truth.

# CHAPTER 2
## THE BIG PUSH

A big push started in the 20th century when we received strong cosmic influences. The effect of these influences was a change in the norms, especially in Western society, and then all over the world. There were world wars and revolutions, including a sexual revolution; cloning (which involves cell division and DNA); globalization; feminist upheavals; the atomic bomb; Ataturk; *The Knowledge Book* and much more. There was physical and emotional pain and suffering, while at the same time, great advances in science and technology and in our consciousness, were taking place.

Pain and suffering can provide incentive for mankind to withdraw from dangerous situations. To understand this concept, we'll read about the influence of new physics and, their description of entropy. In order to comprehend and appreciate life on our planet, it is essential to accept the fact that all things come from a Center that is fed from beyond space-time and completely eludes comprehension.

Take a look at a flower. Its Center is like a storage house of energy whence comes order, design and the energy that sustains the life of the flower. Likewise, it is a Seed that unifies the cell and the Spirit; it unifies all that there is. Therefore, a flower symbolizes Love. It was a Seed that brought atoms and nuclei to the earth and beyond, in order to introduce reproduction and distribute the information to all universes known and still unknown. It is a Seed that keeps universes dying, while others are born, a Seed that inspires our thoughts without surcease. Everyone of us is a flower, composed of six petals connected to our brain. As such, human beings are a symbol of the dimension of Love and Light that reflect to planets, galaxies, universes. Triangles and pyramids, also play a major role in our existence. It is thanks to triangles that light is dispersed in a prismatic form. But, the secret of the universe is manifested in the pyramids. Each of us, humans, are a pyramid, and the secret is within us.

Ponder this: There must have been a Center that is One Nucleus, that started to fragment, leading to the Big

Bang. From that came explosions, causing what is known as nucleuses, which is the plural of nucleus, and this is our world today. There are innumerable other worlds like ours. The conclusion from the Big Bang is that One Nucleus led the way to crude matter in the form of countless particles dispersing all over to a space where there was nothing, yet from which all was created.

It is our mission to return to that One Nucleus.

This event reminds us that our Ultimate Source, The Creator of All Creations, some of us call The Unknown, or God, is beyond the form of a nucleus, as we know it on earth. It is also beyond crude matter and beyond the formation of the Big Bang. It is a reminder that life has always existed in other forms unknown to us, even before the world began. Indeed, before we assume any localized form, on earth or beyond, we go through a myriad of incremental stages of development. Preparatory to being a human, for instance, we may become a blade of grass, a stone, a tree, a spider, a cat. This does not deny the religious books, but rather complements them: we are a magnificent product of the Creator of All Creations' imagination.

Do you know that thoughts are not lost independent of how far they can reach? Are you aware that we are always progressing, especially when we go through pain? Do you realize we are always receiving information from beyond space and time, and always giving it back after we digest it? This is a system that has been set up among many others that we may never know. In spite of the pain, the system cannot be changed, as the truth is that we learn through suffering. We learn from the contrast of opposites. Example: How do you know that you are happy? You must have gone through some form of unhappiness before.

Are you aware that there are billions of particles pouring on us from beyond space and time and that they supply us with all kinds of information? This is ineluctable science going on 24/7.

As previously mentioned, the energy that causes various stages of development comes from the Big Bang as Light. This is when the nucleus started to manifest and Allah, who had received the Power from the Unknown, participated in the application of crude matter with other creators. All is coded and recorded in DNA as in a history book. It contains billions or even trillions of information. But, each of us receives the information gradually. In other words, we are given only what human beings, as a whole, are ready to comprehend and accept in line with its development. This means we receive more advanced information as the whole world progresses, from little pushes to big pushes. It is very important to understand that progress toward unification of the masses starts with each individual. We are a Natural Pyramid, we received Light, we give Light!

CHAPTER 3

## HOW DO WE KNOW WE ARE PROGRESSING?

First of all, it is not up to us to find out the complete answer to this question. The main reason is because, while on earth, we are not aware of the full picture about millions of centuries of existence, and the ongoing cycles of life.

Some of our cells are locked while we are on this planet, so that we do not get the info about our past lives. We'll read more about this topic in the chapter "The Energy Cord." In addition, we can have some knowledge via information received in advance of the events, in the form of reflections.

The question is: Is our level of spiritual maturity high enough so that we may accept such knowledge without fear and wisely act upon it? Or are we cynically laughing at its first intimation, pushing it aside, completely dismissing it and then wondering why we feel depressed? In short do we have an open mind and willpower to overcome our ignorance? Are we afraid of the truth, which is that we are always receiving information from The Beyond? The information comes from Beings that have been on earth and are aware of all sides of our lives; past, present and future. We must realize that we do not take steps because we want to, but because we need to pay our debts to mankind. Among those "giving back" are many examples in the history of the world. However, not all of us want to go public. Some prefer to stay incognito; others produce great works of art that can help humans, if thoughts do not lead them astray.

    For instance, we have the example of Leonardo da Vinci 1452-1519. He had no formal education. Artist, inventor and scientist, he drew human anatomy in great detail before anyone had such knowledge. He also sketched designs for parachutes, airplanes, UFOs. Can you imagine living in the 15th century and receiving such images and detailed info? He is perhaps best known for his portrait *Mona Lisa* (*La Gioconda*). Recently it was discovered that the painting appears to bear hidden images of an alien figure, a secret code, and subliminal messages probably involving extraterrestrials. Furthermore, it is also possible that he used the same technique in other paintings.  The question is: Why did it take so many centuries for mankind to discover such images? It has to do with the fact that perception is related to the way we interpret the truth and mankind has to be prepared as a Whole for that knowledge to be explained to us. This is the task of the brain. In other words, the brain may be anxious to truly clarify our perceptions, but everyone on earth, has to be ready, as a Whole, to accept what is true. And this may be painful to many people who refuse to have an open mind and prefer to live on lies.  Art is a very spiritual medium, many of us know that. However, we may ask: are we acting upon it?

Are we ready to recognize the importance of our thoughts and consciousness, and see that it is necessary to take steps for the benefit of mankind?  This may also be discerned when we listen to Handel's Messiah which is a majestic blend of music and Scripture. Its creator, George Frederic Handel (1685-1759) compose church music from age 11. Although his father wanted him to study law, he refused. He went blind towards the end of his life.

Conventionally regarded as the Father of Science Fiction, Jules Verne (1828-1905) was a novelist, a poet, and playwright. He foretold of airplanes, skyscrapers, submarines, and space travel.

Thomas Edison (1847-1931) had three months of formal education. And yet, assisted by many others, he invented the light bulb, telephone, and motion pictures, receiving more than 1,000 patents.

The 20th century saw many scientists producing great works, such as S. Hawking and Nikola Tesla. Harkening to his inner voices and images, renowned genius Albert Einstein (1879-1955) became famous at the age of 26. That's when he published a paper about what became known as the Theory of Relativity, which describes the structure and interplay of space-time. We were told that a particle of matter can be changed into energy, and vice versa. What he did was to release the atom and was very disappointed with the lack of progress of humanity. Some individuals question the possibility that he was an alien. His famous sentence "oceanic feeling" referring to God and the cosmos is very important for humanity to reflect.

Stephen Hawking (1942-2018) was a theoretical physicist, scientist and cosmologist. *The KB* mentions that he comes from the 79$^{th}$ Dimension. Despite a rare form of Lou Gehrig's disease that paralyzed him for life, the undiminished workings of his phenomenal brain continue to thrill people the world over. He stated that the universe is governed by laws of science.

Nikola Tesla (1856-1943) was a mechanical and electrical engineer, and a futurist inventor best known for his invention of a generator to produce the alternating current of electricity. He never become a businessman, and consequently, other inventors took advantage of him. He – not Marconi -- invented radio, and offered ideas to the US military, but they did not take him seriously. He proposed to build what we know as radar and was rejected by the military as a laughingstock! He died in a hotel in New York City, in poverty.

CHAPTER 4

## THE MILKY WAY AND THE ARTS

On a clear night, whether you are in an arid area, or by the ocean, remember to contemplate the sky. If you see a long strip of what looks like a shredded spiral of light, be aware that you are contemplating our world. Indeed, what you are looking at is an area with a countless number of stars, including our sun, which is also a star. In this space there are also many planets, and our planet earth is but one of them. The area is a galaxy known as the Milky Way because of the effect of Light on the sky.

It is a haughty illusion to imagine that we are alone. We exist in the Milky Way together with many other planets and with Beings with different physical features, as well as more advanced levels of thought. We may call them extraterrestrials; they regard us as small insects.

We forget that although our temporary physical form is crude matter, one day we'll be beyond the physical, beyond the terrestrial. The truth is that there is no death; thoughts and consciousness do not die: they are interminable, whether in physical form or not we'll have to handle them. We'll always go back to where we came from. We also forget that there is the possibility of the existence of parallel universes, and that we may live in a multiple universe.

While we are aware that we exist on earth, all events in our lives may be repeated in reverse in other worlds but we do not know what form we will take. In any case, this confirms what we read before, that thinking is interminable. Still, its form changes as we progress towards the Light.

Why do we forget? Is it fear of the so-called Unknown?

We do not realize that we are trapped in our own planet and need to get out. Many of us still imagine that this is the only planet and that there is only one life for us to live on earth. Fortunately, once in a blue moon, some of us feel we are in Heaven; the reality is that accordance with what is written, we are in both Heaven or hell, depending on our stage of spiritual development.

Our level of thought is mainly the evolutionary scale known as the Third Dimension (height, width, length), because we block the knowledge of other dimensions. This makes it hard to open up our wings, so to speak, and fly to other dimensions. It also makes it hard for us to accept the existence of other lifeforms that have more advanced technology than we; where 2+2 is not 4, but can be 12, 16 or higher, in accordance with their frequencies and form of measurement.

But we should not put ourselves down. For millions of years we, the biological robots, have accumulated a great deal of knowledge, which is clearly accelerating. Much of this knowledge has been repressed and will remain so until mankind is ready to open the immensity of it all, including their past lives.

We have learned a great deal during our many lives on earth. How was this knowledge acquired? Through joy, pain and suffering, which are the essential provocations of the system that has been designed for us.

The purpose of our many lives on earth is to help humans collectively improve their thoughts and consciousness, so that we can awake as a whole and return to our former unity with the Unknown. Consequently, we do not have to fly anywhere, but rather use our thoughts to turn inward and allow our cells to open up, so that the information accumulated there can be activated and contribute to our progress in our present form on earth.

In order to achieve these dramatic changes, we need to be provoked in such a way that we choose to discipline ourselves. For that reason, the words in *The Text* are charged with a technique unknown to mankind and described as a particle of light force known as a Photon, moving at a speed that we, on earth, cannot measure. This information may confuse readers since we are not used to forms of measurement from the Celestial Beings. Furthermore, we cannot expect their words, terms, expressions to be like ours. For instance, as previously mentioned, their form of measurement depends on their frequency: It is called Micron. This is why in their dimensions 2x2 is not 4. It may be 14, 16 or more.

It is necessary to understand that our frequency is low because we restrict our thoughts to the Third Dimension. Therefore, the higher the dimension our thoughts take us to, the higher is our frequency to the point that our thoughts create universes. It should be no surprise to read that Stephen Hawking was from the 79$^{th}$ dimension.
Light speeds are also different. The power of the Photons are equivalent to the entire speed of matter and also Cosmic energy which is light and part of the Spiritual Plan. Here we have a dance between the two energies: material and spiritual. Here we imagine the power of the power of attraction.

In the end, the speed of the Photon is beyond dimensions. It is a Power that unites all cosmic power. It is breath, it is not energy: It is from the Divine. This Photon itself opposes our form of thinking and this is how our transformation begins, as our thoughts, in the 3$^{rd}$ dimension, will advance to other horizons.

Of course, our thoughts will go on, but in a different form, which is beyond the terrestrial.

Do not be disturbed because our form of thinking, which is based on separation, was created at the Big Bang as a result of the two universes: positive and negative. Here we have the confirmation that we came from a singleness that split into two. Now we need to unify. As we'll read later on, even our thoughts will be modified when our consciousness is unified as one.

Who can attract this Power? Human beings with advanced thought system.

If we accept, or at least try to understand that we can use logic and reason, we become aware of our potential to liberate our thoughts to new horizons. This way, we can free ourselves from the thoughts of the world, our third dimension, and start to think in an entirely new form. Then, we can absorb Light instead of darkness. Light is where we are heading: we came from Light, we have to go back to Light.

This is the century for provocations activated by the ego.

Some of us are aware that the ego is also a messenger from The Beyond and it is all planned as a system to help us become perfect human beings while we are still embodied. We see how this is manifested in the news, in politics, in our families, on the internet, in our jobs, in short, everywhere. Provocations can also lead to conspiracies which are plans that cause harm in all aspects of our lives.

It is no longer just the individual's progress that matters; it is the collective's, as a Whole. This is why the media, such as mass communication, TV, newspapers etc. was invented, and this is why the concept of "global" became so important recently. Anyhow, it will take centuries to materialize.

When we provoke, we must be aware of the need to respect others and take responsibility for our actions. It is true that, at this stage in the history of the world, humans provoke humans, perhaps more than ever. In the next chapter, we'll read about a well-known provoker. But we must realize that in the end it is our thought system that promotes provocations within ourselves, which are then manifested in the outer world.

We have the example of Stephen Hawking. He announced that planets with beings like us exist but they are not found in large numbers. This conclusion caused him to be provoked. In this case, he was verbally criticized by the media and even by fellow scientists, few of whom recognized that he was an image, a reflection of the potential of all human brains. I am sure he used the provocations to inspire his research until the end of his life. What he did was to reverse the provocations he received and this is a great lesson that all of us must consider.

At this stage in human evolution, we must realize that even provocations are part of the spiritual plan that facilitates our return to our Source.
Of course, most of the time, we are not aware of what we are doing, and why. Are we alone in reacting to these provocations? Absolutely not. We are never alone.
A Loving Energy far beyond words and understanding is always with us, guiding us, and opening our eyes to new

knowledge. Nevertheless, to accept that information, we must have achieved a certain development in consciousness. And for that reason, we receive cosmic energies from beyond space and time that incline us to react positively or negatively, depending on our evolutionary stage. These energies inspire us to admire trees, birds, flowers, and all of nature. Once under its influence, we find ourselves connected to our heart.

Unaware of the underlying reason for what is happening, we are moved to creative pursuits – painting, sculpting, designing jewelry, compose music, writing books and poems. This is when we realize we are all artists.

We know that regardless of the particular medium, art has to do with our involvement with public consciousness. It elevates us to the Beyond.

Leonardo da Vinci never went to school. Picasso disliked formal education, He even avoided it. These famous artists were not influenced by any school of thought, but by their own minds and hearts. All of us can do the same; we can become the artists of our own lives, if we allow our consciousness to attract the power of Light.

## CHAPTER 5
## WHO IS THE MOST FAMOUS OF ALL PROVOKERS? DEVIL, OF COURSE

As we proceed, we'll discover interesting and provocative references to the devil (ego, Satan, Lucifer). It is considered that he/she/it has no difficulty evaluating our needs. This means that in the end, the devil is very shrewd and sometimes very quick. We learn that Adam and Eve were manifested on earth together with the devil. The purpose of Adam and the devil was to protect Eve. Of course, we know that Adam had another purpose.

It is mentioned in the chapter titled "The Milky Way and the Arts" that provocations materialize in the world as per our own thoughts.

Let's recall that all of us – including the devil --were created with a purpose, and a mission. As we have read, all things are one inside the other. That means that the devil is inside us. Good and bad are part of a system known as thermodynamics and presented in another chapter.

In spite of the fact that the devil was expelled from Heaven, we should not see him as an enemy, but rather as part of the thought system that has been implemented on earth in order to help us. The aim is to increase humans' awareness of the need to undo negativity, based on the truths that we are learning about.

We must continuously renew our choice to use knowledge and logic instead. Furthermore, we must also consider that our negative thoughts are sent back to us because they are blocked and cannot go through a specific area to achieve resolution and help us advance. This is what fuels our depressions: we keep repeating the same mistakes and therefore succumb to their influence.

Should we appreciate the devil's mission?
Let's reflect on this question. Maybe, with some effort on our part, we will realize that because of his provocations, the devil gives us opportunities to handle our thoughts in new ways that can help us harmoniously unify, if we so choose. In the end, the devil is a learning tool.

Let's invite him to do exactly what we're trying to do -- that is, transcend negativity. It has been written that there is no love in the devil. But we can also imagine there is no love in some of us, and that is part of our dream. Although love is everywhere we can hide it and even dismiss it; our mission is planned that way whereas, the devil's mission was planned so that he had to be expelled from Heaven.

    What happened to us? Were we also expelled from Heaven? Absolutely not! Heaven is in our hearts. Heaven can be right here and right now, it all depends on our thoughts. A loving God would not expel us from where He knows we belong: Heaven. What we know is that our consciousness is split. All events were planned as a reminder to mankind that we must expel from ourselves all negative thoughts, such as those of fear, envy and hate. In the advanced state of Heaven, there is no opposition, no need for establishing equilibrium. There is only True-Love. By the time we get to that advanced stage, which can be right now and right here, while on earth, all our negative thoughts will have been transmuted via our experiences in the laboratory known as life on earth.

Our rage, anger, hate and jealousy can reach us only from a non-loving source, which is our little self. Call it devil, Satan, ego, or whatever you wish. Its purpose is to bring us fear and retard our progress towards unification of consciousness.

But we can reverse our thoughts. Love is the creative energy of the Creator of All Creations and does not discriminate. Like the sun, it shines equally on both sinner and saint. Unfortunately, many of us have closed our hearts to Love.

What this means is that all of us on earth have been trying to unite Allah's Plan which has to do with crude matter, with the Creator of All Creators' Plan that is, The Unknown, which has to do with Spirit. This is being achieved through reincarnations and love is always involved as described in the next chapter titled "The On-going Cycles of Life."

We do not return to earth by force but because we choose to. However, as noted, we are generally unaware of what we are doing and too often we fall when we are tempted.

In the Bible, Luke 4:5-8, we have an example of how Jesus was tempted by the devil, and how He reacted to the temptation.

"Then the devil, taking Him up on a high mountain, showed Him all the kingdoms of the world in a moment of time. And the devil said to Him," All this authority I will give You, and their glory; for *this* has been delivered to me, and I give it to whomever I wish. Therefore, if you worship before me, all will be Yours."

And Jesus answered him and said to Him, "" Get behind Me, Satan! For it is written, "" You shall worship the Lord your God, and Him only you shall serve.""

In this exchange, we see how patient Jesus is with the system we have created. He did not tell the devil to go to hell and leave Him alone. He told him to step behind Him and watch how His thoughts unfolded right before the devil's eyes.

Jesus let His heart rule Him. What he did was to undo the devil's provocation.

This method of Satan's provocation is part of Allah's Plan and his hierarchy of creators; the aim is to lead mankind into error with the purpose to give us exams so that we look unto our consciousness and open up to the truth.

Such an example of leading mankind into error is manifested in the above quote: "All this authority I give you and their glory…"

Then, we have the Spiritual Plan which ratifies the knowledge also as per above quote; "Therefore if you worship before me, all will be yours." This affirmation gave Jesus a choice of whom to worship. And this choice applies to all humans independent of any religion, or cultural background.

We have read that thoughts travel to the Beyond, for better or for worse, and certainly Jesus knew where His thoughts travelled to. He knew about the power of Reflections and the Divine.

Too many of us adore the devil, but please do not prostrate.

CHAPTER 6
## THE ONGOING CYCLES OF LIFE
## THE THREAD AND THE SPOOL

Some of us are beginning to accept and understand that life existed on other planets before the world began. This means that there was life before sex, that is, before the nucleus, and there will be life after sex. There is a Thought independent of our physical form. Interestingly enough that Thought is ongoing and leads us through many stages of our development. This also means that the coding of DNA by the genes was planned long before the world began, before Adam and Eve, before the fetus and the womb. It was planned at a time beyond what we know as time, when our thoughts and consciousness were unified in a totality beyond our imagination. Therefore, there was no need to prepare codes, but the time was right to start planning.

At whatever level we are in our development, a Great Intelligence is always present to show us the way to continue to live.

This takes us to the question of what happened at the Big Bang. In any event, it was a symbol of gestation and birth, in the sense that a burst came from inwards, from a unified Whole that exploded, caused fire and spread outward, emanating countless particles. In other words, separation of a unified consciousness was manifested in a space where there was nothing but all was created including a countless number of galaxies, our planet and us.

As a result of this event, the Big Bang conveys the image of humans' consciousness disintegrating and its particles running away from its Origin, its Home. Still, we never let go of the source of the Fire. When that happened we were lost, like babies, in a new environment and on the verge of extinction if we did not have a Loving Invisible Power to take care of us. Indeed, Love saved us! Spirals were created to hold us together, to help us find balance, to unify and recover our consciousness. The Truth is that the universe was born spinning, so was our salvation. This was a great triumph of technology and science before our existence. May we ask then if God is a scientist?

> "Science without religion is lame;
> Religion without science is blind."
> Albert Einstein

Did Creation stop at the spirals? Absolutely not. The truth is that Creation never stops. The Law of Cause and Effect is always in effect. We are here, now, preparing to go back. Life cycles will go on and on for centuries. Reincarnations will go on as long as we choose. We'll return again and again, creating in what looks like endless cycles copying and repeating the same events. As a consequence of the Big Bang, many more Big Bangs will happen. The nucleus, the spirals, the atoms, crude matter -- all will be formed as copies of their past. As it is written in the Old Testament, "There is nothing new under the sun."

In a very distant future, another centrifugal universe, like ours, will be created and our planet will be reborn.

We have read that the universe was born spinning around a specific axis, the mission of which is to direct the nucleus, and hold it within a certain order.

The First Constitution and Law of Universes was prepared beyond Times with the participation of many entities in a dimension known as Atlanta,(a mystical nation mentioned in Plato's Dialogues about 350BC).

In other words, particles sharing the same thoughts worked as a whole to transfer their thoughts to form planets and us.

It is also written that Atlanta Dimension was populated by androgynous Beings called Atlanteans, and that the human body is a prototype of Atlanta, because Adam was from that Dimension. And that is why he had to have an operation to produce Eve. Then, billions of centuries later, the same rules and regulations were initiated on our planet, in a new environment that had been specially designed for the earth to start life again via reproduction through the nucleus.

Coming back to what we think is a new world, we have played this game many times. However, it is a replica of the past, just as we are copies of preexisting forms: we are prototypes. All of us are born with a mission; some of us are born to destroy, others to joyously build, like children making castles in the sand. Indeed, we are created with the potential to love and to hate: The choice is ours! Let's remember that we have free will. Are we ready to accept that before Adam and Eve, life came from other forms that were created before the nucleus? This esoteric assumption makes many researchers realize that their job is impossible since the beginning and the end are entangled; but we are not aware of this. Like the mythic Ouroboros, the snake that swallows its own tale to sustain itself, the earth too undergoes endless cycles of renewal. We are not aware that universes exist one inside the other, and that religion and learning are also one inside the other. In the end what this means is that separation is an illusion invented by humans, before we became humans.

Due to the advances of science, mankind has learned that DNA also contains information about interaction with different species that occurred in our development, as well as with beings before our own system of reproduction was initiated. Therefore, vestigial features of those very old species and Beings exist within all of us. Indeed, all of us are on the same boat, navigating with an invisible captain.

The 3rd dimension (our world) contributes to the ongoing cycles of life. All is connected and always will be. Again, let's remember that all things are one inside the other. Somehow, they are unified! All contributes to the ongoing cycles of life. It is therefore fitting that we love a stone, a flower, an animal, a human being, and all of Creation. We are bound to cause and effect, as well as reincarnation as we keep repeating the same events that have been recorded while we are in the box of our 3rd dimension. This is the reason why we have to open the box, get out and go to higher dimensions.

Eventually, we'll be going beyond dimensions, beyond galaxies, beyond Omega which is the exit of terrestrial love and the entrance of Divine Love. This is the cosmic journey that mankind is undertaking. It started with the hardships of the First Cosmic Age, the 20th century, which will end with the 3rd Cosmic Age, the 22nd century. Therefore, we are given three centuries to prepare the foundation for the New Golden Age.

Do not be disappointed. Appreciate the chance humanity is having now to understand why we need to take the necessary steps to advance.

Understand also the power of cosmic influences we are receiving now from Omega's reflections which prepare the foundations for the New Golden Age. Although such influences may be painful at times, they are a sign of progress achieved by mankind. Then, life on earth will became easier. In the meantime, we are being helped and protected by the Celestial Beings.

It is explained that even scientific research done on earth has not helped mankind to understand what we are going through.

The concept of time and the repetition of the ongoing cycles, may be understood by those of us who enjoy sewing and or knitting. Besides thread, we need a needle and spool. Let's imagine that the spool is full and represents time. In this case it represents centuries of civilizations on earth that have been taped and rolled up. When the cycle ends, the spool is empty. As new cycles are formed, the spool starts to rewind again. We need more thread. We repeat the events many times, as we go through our many life cycles. Our learning goes on: we keep repeating and repeating.

    Do we recognize how damaging these ongoing cycles are for humanity and how much our guides try to help us? We are always being helped even in the most difficult and unexpected circumstances. It is also understood that Love is always present. We repeat the same events and may get in trouble again and again, while we are not aware that he Unknown always forgives us.

    In the midst of our ordeals, we are still receiving shock waves from the explosion of the Big Bang which have killed dolphins in contact with water. These waves may also be called waves of Resurrection. They help us awake and remember that the Thought mentioned at the beginning of this chapter is always with us, and that our knowledge is primitive because we block our thought expansion.

    Furthermore, we need to open our minds to other possibilities beyond the terrestrial, including considering that other beings who exist in other galaxies, may also need to understand love and attain a unified consciousness.

Mankind will be advancing when we realize that our visit to this planet is very limited in space and time and when we accept that our thoughts are ongoing independent of our physical body. Cosmic waves of resurrection also help us accept that our thoughts have consequences and that life expresses in a myriad of forms, independent of how and where they are reproduced. In the meantime, we must realize that we are not alone, and above all we are a copy, an image, a reflection of the genuine Love of the Creator.

In short, the cosmic waves of resurrection are helping us advance to a more fulfilling and harmonious life on earth.

It is clear that when mankind accepts the fact our knowledge is primitive because we block its thought expansion; when all of us open our minds to other possibilities beyond the terrestrial; when we accept and understand that our thoughts are ongoing and have consequences independent of our physical body; when we accept that life expresses in a myriad forms, independent of how and where it is reproduced; that is when we will be advancing to a more fulfilling and peaceful life on earth.

Then we'll get rid of our terrestrial thoughts through the exit door of Omega and proceed to the opening gate of the Divine which is also Omega's. In other words, we'll cross the road from terrestrial love, and enter the road to Divine Love.

CHAPTER 7
# SEX AND LOVE
# OMEGA'S MISSION

Would you believe that love can be terrestrial and Divine, whereas sex is only terrestrial? If we say we love birds, we certainly do not expect sex to be involved. The first concepts and expressions of love had nothing to do with sex. It was simply natural to be united as One before our planet was created. Indeed, at that time, the thought of Love had nothing to do with physical bodies but with our single consciousness as a *Whole*. Hopefully humans are on the verge of accepting the fact that there are Beings living on other planets where their form of reproduction differs from ours. It has to do with their thought forms and attempt to unify consciousness.

Whereas while on our planet, our form of reproduction was specifically designed to be achieved through the union of two people, so that human beings would experience earthly love, leading to True-Love and go through the exit door of our terrestrial thoughts.

It is written that in the bodily union of two people, our awareness increases;

we are in control of mind and body, we are connected to the earth, and the sexual discharge becomes very important. As a matter of fact, the energy spent in those final moments is equivalent to the energy of a universe. It is this energy that helps the unborn unify their energies. The problem is that many of us see this union as love of the flesh and are not aware, or refuse to accept that it is love of that Unknown energy that created us and is even beyond what we know as energy. Therefore, strong sexual emotions have nothing to do with sex; they are spiritual.

Remember this sentence: The forces that we cannot see but keep us together are spiritual.

There are many Beings that want to be embodied and are waiting for their turn as they watch the parents they have chosen: this is why two people always feel the need for someone else, in this case an infant.

Can you imagine the pressure put on the parents from the Invisible Forces and also from the unborn himself/herself who wants desperately to be born and that event may be delayed? This is the reason why I have forgiven my parents: I know I've chosen them. The reader can do the same, and apply the same concept to all events and people you meet. All relationships, good or bad, have been previously chosen with a specific purpose to be achieved. This is the truth, which may be hard for some of us to accept, while for others it may be seen as a blessing.

It is necessary for human beings to realize the importance of sexual relations and the power of the invisible forces. Let's never forget that if the Thought of Love is not involved we are violating the rules of All Creators. We know that Light conveys information which is knowledge and leads to consciousness.

In Genesis we read about the creation of Adam and Eve, which brought procreation to the earth. We also read about the existence of androgynous beings that had the characteristics of both sexes. Their method of procreation was probably based on their advanced thought system, and their connection to the Divine, so that beings were manifested without any physical contact. Adam was one of them. As such he had to be split into "two" in order to satisfy our predesigned way of life and bring Eve to life. As in cell division, one made two! After that traumatic "operation," Adam was put to sleep and evidently, has not yet awakened!

This event is rendered symbolically to remind all of us of our present condition. Indeed, we were all put to sleep, the moment we imagined that we ran away from our *single* consciousness, abandoning our union with the Invisible Force. This was physically manifested by the Big Bang explosion when our Oneness fragmented and two universes were created: positive and negative---the twin universe. This is the reason why duality exists everywhere; in science, in religion, in every aspect of our lives.

In the 20$^{th}$ century, scientists concluded that when we are fetuses, there is no discernible distinction between male and female; that sexual identity comes later as we continue to develop in the womb. As we have read, our formation is based on a prototype that is, a copy of the androgynous. Then we gradually changed as we adapted to our earthly needs. The adaptation was performed by a Great Scientist who exists beyond the earth and in our hearts.

It was The Creator's Love and longing for us to return to our previous state of unity that created Adam and Eve.

Human beings need to remember that Two can make One, but One can also make Two and herein lies the power of the Divine. Our thoughts and our hearts always play a major role in all events occurring on the earth and beyond. Only an Unknown Great Invisible Power could have created these technological and scientific marvels with a precision beyond words and comprehension. This happened so that we may be able to go through the exit gate of Omega. Then, we proceed on our way out of terrestrial love to Omega's entrance gate of Divine love.

That's Omega's mission; one gate is the exit of our terrestrial thoughts, the other is the entrance gate to the Divine. Omega always supervises all our energies.

CHAPTER 8

## **THE TWIN UNIVERSE
(A GHOST)**

Adam and Eve were set up to perform a mission already scientifically and technologically organized in an artificial world for which they were prepared in advance. In other words, all events were carefully rehearsed in an unknown area especially designed for such a rehearsal, just like the scenes of a play.

We learn for the first time in human history that after the rehearsal is completed the information reflects to a second universe, which existed before the earth and where the first encounter of Adam and Eve materialized (we can imagine the First Universe being the Universe of Light).

Let's recall that Light conveys information and knowledge.
In any case, the Light coming from the $1^{st}$ Universe reflected on another area which became the first biological universe known as the $2^{nd}$ Second Universe. It was manifested by a physical contact between a man and a woman, that is between Adam and Eve and the birth of many Adams and Eves.

Then as the information continued to reflect, Adam and Eve worked to form our planet, in a Natural Area, where there are many worlds.

To recap:

A) The first universe is the Universe of Light. From there all reflects to all there is, was and will be created.

B) All events prior to being manifested anywhere, are rehearsed in an artificial area.

C) Afterwards this information is reflected in a Second Universe, where Adam and Eve had their first encounter. And that is the reason why the Second Universe became known as the First Biological Universe.

D) All of this happened before the formation of our Planet.

E) Then Adam and Eve worked to establish an area where our Planet was formed. For that reason, our Planet is like a ghost, a twin: everything that happens here is a reflection of what happened before.

Therefore, our universe is a mirror of a twin universe, also known as parallel universe. While our universe, which is positive, moves forward; The other, which is negative, moves backwards.

The concept of twin universes existed even before the formation of the earth. Here, again, we have the confirmation that all is connected, and will always be. Furthermore, reflections played a major part in our lives before and after our formation.

Now the question is: Did sex start with Adam and Eve? First of all, we are aware that thoughts come before actions. Therefore, sex starts with a Thought from beyond space and time, and is followed by action. As it is mentioned in the 1$^{st}$ Chapter, consciousness is a form of thought and cannot be separated. This was manifested for the first time by the union of Adam and Eve, as we know. Much later, it reflected on the earth and other planets in different ways.

This means that our planet, known as the Third Dimension, inherited the experience of sex, based on physical coupling from Adam and Eve. But, this type of experience is temporary. It endures only while we are in our present physical form on our planet.

Herein lies the design of sexual intercourse, which pertains to the Third Dimension only: Its real message is to help us remember that all things are one inside the other; there is no separation and this is the meaning of Wholeness, Unity and Love.

We may still ask: what else is there to find out about sex? Do not be surprised when you read that the "Fourth Dimension" which is the state we call heaven, right after we dispose of our physical bodies, is also biological. This means that we still have some form of a body but with other characteristics, as it is described in the chapter titled "Heaven."

Besides, in other dimensions children are conceived without physical contact. They are manifested through Thoughts, so that we begin to realize the importance of Thinking and our relationship with the Divine.

Can the reader relate this concept to the birth of Christ?

Again, this is a sign that our universe is a twin.

Such events are necessary so that we correct our lack of love and the mistakes we made while on earth. Many of us, need another chance to be together in a different environment and in different circumstances, beyond the earth. This happens so that we experience peace and love which we were not able to attain in our previous life on this planet with the relationships we had. Then, after we experience joy, harmony, fulfillment, make amendments and atone, we finally dispose of our biological bodies. Again, we'll read more details about our journey in the chapter titled "Heaven.".

Reflect on this: If you think that you got rid of your wife or husband or, any other relationship while on earth and still hold grudges against them, you will be surprised to find out that you may meet that person again in heaven, and beyond.

Why?

We have read that we are always learning whether we are in physical form or not. Once in the $4^{th}$ dimension, we begin to realize that Love predominates and it is where we will make amends. Again, the purpose is for us to realize the importance of our thoughts, and our

relationship with the Divine, and for that reason we have Beings beyond space and time assisting us in our ordeals.
This is the game duality plays in our lives while we are on earth and even beyond until our consciousness unifies.
Perhaps this is the reason why the Photon at such a great speed that cannot be measured on earth, was established at this time in human history. The Celestial Beings that implemented the system hope that we may be able to extend our thoughts to the infinite while on earth as well as beyond. We can start practicing now and have a taste of happiness.

    Herein lies the eternal power of the union of Thought of the Created with the Creator. The saga continues.

# CHAPTER 9
## "I THINK, THEREFORE I AM"
### Rene Descartes
### French Philosopher and Man of Science (1596-1650)

As we proceed, we may wonder at the way Photons are established which cannot be measured on earth. We imagine a photon to be a particle of Light. But we learn that from the beginning, it was an electromagnetic force that was activated before the Big Bang, and contributed to the formation of Light, fire, and sound.

Today, it is thanks to that "force" that we are able to advance our thought system.

Because of the tremendous speed of the photon and its power of attraction, of which we are not even aware, the time we spend thinking is reduced drastically. This happens as we go on reading. We do not waste our thoughts but use them constructively. As a consequence of this process, our consciousness advances faster than we can imagine. What happens is that *Powers* that we are not familiar with, are loaded on the letters of the Text.

This may be considered a mystery for now, but in the future, it will not be. As such, all of us are protected. The protection extends not only to those who are given the permission to read, but also to those who were chosen to write *it* by hand. It takes about one year to handwrite and that is an exciting experience especially when we don't understand most of what we are writing.

As a consequence of our experiences, we arrive at the conclusion that humans must stop blaming each other; we have no power to stop events. The only power we have is to stop wasting our brains.

Just those five words in Descartes' quote shed light on the world. The only knowledge he decided to seek, he found within himself. Then, he concluded:
"I think, therefore I am."
He, of course, also concluded that he existed!

Like many philosophers and religious writers, Descartes served as precursor to *The Knowledge Book.* Besides being a philosopher, he worked on the use of coordinates in

mathematics. He also stressed the importance of logic, truth, reason, morals, metaphysics and conscious experience. These are some of the areas we too must embrace as we journey to perfect personhood. In other words, we need to use logic, to reason and to be aware, among other efforts.
Descartes was a devout Catholic and hoped that one day we would understand that God is science.

There is another aspect to his famous quote. It has to do with the continuation of life after death and therefore, reincarnation.
He did not say,

> "I think, therefore I exist but only when I am in a body."

We know about the influence of our thoughts. Descartes knew that thoughts are ongoing, whether we are embodied or not. On the other hand, he had no proof of other forms of life in galaxies like we have today.

In some of those galaxies, there are beings who once lived on earth and are now abroad UFOs, observing us. One of them identifies himself as Bertrand Russell, the British philosopher

(1872-1970), as described in another chapter.

Again, we arrive at the same conclusion that all is connected. For millions or even trillions of centuries, in an endless whirlpool of events, the world has been materialized by our thoughts. But we forget. If Descartes were among us today, he would patiently read *The KB* and perhaps, once he had a glimpse of its contents, see its similarity to his conclusions.

## CHAPTER 10
### WHERE DO THOUGHTS COME FROM?

Some of the questions posed in previous chapters may lead the reader to inquire more deeply into where do thoughts come from?

Who or what supplies the thoughts to a human, an animal, a flower, a tree? A sunflower, for instance, makes a cracking sound at sunset when it closes and again at sunrise when it opens. I watched this great event many times in my backyard when I was a child.

The truth is that an Extraordinary Power and Invisible Energy supplies "The Thought" to All Creations under any circumstances.

"The universe begins to look more like A Great Thought than a great machine."
James Jeans—The Mysterious Universe

Indeed, planet earth was specially designed so that all living things experience thoughts of crude matter, Spirit, sex and Love.

It is a great privilege to be created the way we are. However, sex does not exist for the sake of sex. It exists for the sake of the Love, that created us!

Reflect on this: When two people unite they receive and give universal energies from the "Beyond," which we cannot even begin to understand for now.

We read in the First Chapter that Light is the source of our thoughts; it is knowledge, consciousness and awareness.
It is the mission of DNA to transfer all information to the earth.

Satisfaction of the sexual urge is fun for some people however, it may be dangerous if they seek only fleshy sensations and ego gratification and there is no love. The act of its aftermath may even include emotions of physical violence. It is suggested that sooner or later, we have to realize that enough is enough and that there is more to life than sex. As a matter of (seemingly surprising) fact, it is even suggested that we stop procreating.

Whether we believe it or not during sex, as at all times, an invisible energy is always available to guide us if we ask for help. This applies to everything we do.

However, in our deep sleep, we have little or no awareness of this truth.

Plato, who lived about 400 years before Christ, observed that we drink from the river of oblivion. But it is always possible to wake up. Our unique design equips us to dig deep into the cosmic well until we discover the truth about ourselves.

As previously mentioned, it was Love in the form of spiral waves that saved us from extinction. It is also Love that helps us to awaken. Consequently, during our formation, the job of the nucleus was to structure us physically and mentally through the atom according to DNA. How this is accomplished through Love is considered a mystery. But it should not be, if we realize the Power of The Creator. We know that fundamentally, there is only One Creator. However, we also know now that, on earth, there is a hierarchy of Creators that leads mankind to the One. Again, names, are but symbols. Although many of us do not recognize the workings of cause and effect, our lives are perfect expressions of it. Some choose to throw reason and responsibility to the winds and refuse to face our consciousness.

On the other hand, all is very well planned. We need to go through periodic revolutions so that we may correct our thoughts. The past, especially our very distant past, may be buried and inaccessible to us, but the events in our lives are happening right now, so that as we look at our present actions and thoughts, we may notice intimations of the past and the future. All of us are receiving the fruits of whatever actions we have taken perhaps even millions of years ago. And these fruits may be bitter or sweet. This can be manifested especially in the intimate relations of two people. Anyhow, we are not generally aware of the importance and purpose of the union.

We have yet to be aware that our consciousness is unfolding and that thoughts and impressions are always being filtered. In other words, thoughts are channeled and directed to proceed somewhere so that they are recorded, even during sex. Thoughts come from our Source and are shared with all there is.

We already know it was Love for us that inspired the use of spiral waves, so that we can awaken and eventually return to our Source. This brings us to the point that there are several concepts of love tailored to our stage of development and serving us until all beings develop their thought system in a way that they accomplish their mission on earth in a harmonious way.

## CHAPTER 11
## LOVE

As it is written in chapter 5, Love is creative energy of the Creator of all Creations and does not discriminate.

Love is known to be such a vibration that an emotional state is involved. Earthquakes are a good example for us to identify vibrations. Just like in nature, the electromagnetic fields within us have an influence on our emotional state. We can influence others and vice versa. We can fall in love, and or out of love. There are many concepts of terrestrial love: love of nature, love of country, love of parents, love of humans.

What about inhabitants of other galaxies? We have read that some do not have the notion of love. That is why they need our cooperation so that they receive the reflections of love and understanding that we will provide them with our thought system. This is also the reason why Allah will leave us in the future and goes to other dimensions. Then, on earth, we have the love of God which is beyond the terrestrial.

In the end, all concepts of love lead us to evolvement and purification. How long it may take for us to purify, depends on the road we choose to travel.

The formation of our planet as crude matter happened very close to our Source and this caused our energy to be stronger and more potent than we may realize, plus the fact that our planet is used as a school. It should be no surprise to find out that beings from other galaxies come to earth to experience crude matter, spirit, sex and also genuine and fake love. All of us have the knowledge necessary to progress, but we may find it hard to remember. However, as previously mentioned, humans must be aware that the opportunity for sex as it is performed on earth is unique. This awareness may not be beneficial, especially for those individuals who do not believe in reincarnation and are always preoccupied with their sexual relationships. Presuming that the present life is the only chance they will get to have sex or even to live, their preoccupation is understandable. This misunderstanding may create chaos in their families, friends, the environment and above all, in themselves.

Hopefully, such obsessions are exhausted sooner or later and we end up giving and receiving Authentic Love. In our strife, we recognized that we are not alone, and that there is life after sex. Even if we have a partner, we start seeing him or her as a friend. We begin to let our heart lead us, not our head. We begin to allow reason and logic to guide us. We begin to love ourselves, without being selfish. This can happen especially as we age; it is, in fact, the great value of aging: We recognize that we are the Light. We recognize the need to amend, and the need for grace. Forgiveness leads us; We have no ego. We expect nothing from the recipient of our love. This is unconditional Love. This is True-Love

Finally, there is a transcendent concept: The Love of God, which cannot be described in words. It exists everywhere, in all Galaxies, Universes, Planets; it embraces all there is, in spite of fact that it is not recognized by most of us, on earth and even beyond. But it may be experienced for less than an instant, under certain circumstances, especially when the heart rules.

## CHAPTER 12
### WHEN THE HEART RULES

There are many examples in history of what happens when the heart rules and logic and awareness take over. One of them is the story of a French teenager Joan of Arc who became a warrior and later a saint.

She lived in the 15$^{th}$ century, during the One Hundred Years' War with England. Joan heard voices in her head from French saints and organized an army to fight the British. Her aim was to return France to its people. The church condemned her for not following the Bible and for being inspired by saintly voices rather than by their narrow conception of God.

Joan was charged with heresy and burned at the stake in 1431.If this event had happened today, in the 21$^{st}$ century, may be history would have been different if the importance of reflections had been understood. Indeed, what Joan heard were reflections of thoughts from beyond space and time that had been prepared for her far in advance. Her cosmic journey to the Unknown had both examples of what we call destiny and even luck. If we choose, we follow instructions and guidance prescribed for us far in advance in accordance with our needs, of which we are not aware. Often, we ask ourselves: Is this human? Is this person in her/his right mind? Did Joan choose to burn at stake? It is hard to believe that she may have chosen.

First, we have to consider that we are always under supervision, whether we are on earth or not. Before we come to earth we look at our past lives, and together with our Guides we design the events in our next life. But our actions sometimes do not dependent of our desires, but on what was prearranged by the Celestial Beings in collaboration with us.

Anyone interested in the history of what we may call chaotic human minds, should read about her life and times and also reflect on the fact that history repeats itself. It's astonishing to see how French nationals became friends with the British, which led to her murder.
During her trial, important documents disappeared. The courts were prepared in advance to condemn her. The fact that she was abused just before her death by

some authority figure who visited her cell, is erased from history. The fact that people noticed that her face had been disfigured when she was on her way to be burned is also missing from history. Even some French church members who took advantage of the chaos in France became pro-English and joined in her condemnation.

Perhaps the most interesting aspect of her life is the fact that Joan was guided by what we call energies beyond our imagination. These energies helped her promote events, such as successful battles, and also led to what we call miracles in her short life.

Overall, she too was wholly focused on the reflections of Love. It was her love that saved France from the British and hopefully saved her in the eyes of God, in spite of her many enemies. This is what happens when the heart rules: We save ourselves through suffering and realize that we have to live by opposites.

This is a Law that cannot be changed. And yet, a pressing question still stands: Why would grown-ups and presumably, responsible individuals, condemn a teenager to death? Was it just politics? Was it their misunderstanding of True-Love? Joan had more energy, Love, and Spirit than most of her countrymen. Those who condemned her must have wondered how it was possible that someone so young could be so much more powerful than they.

    Therefore, we may conclude that hatred, jealousy and even fear of Love, led to her condemnation. Throughout her leadership, Joan was a threat to their egos; their jealous eyes could not see her love for France. Indeed, as it was then and continues to be now; humanity's lack of understanding of genuine Love is the cause of misery and chaos in the world.

    The concepts of Love, described in another chapter, apply to life on earth. They underlie the steps necessary for us to progress and to awaken. Suffering is also necessary, as already mentioned since the system is set up this way. We now understand that beyond these concepts, there is the Love of God which is beyond words. Our concepts of love, serve as rungs to the top of the ladder, which no one can ascend overnight. We need several lifetimes to awaken and return to our former unity: this is accomplished in stages, like climbing a ladder. Very often, in desperate moments, we think there is no Love, that it does not exist, that it has disappeared. Eventually we see that the question is not what happened to Love, the question is: What Happened to Humanity?

## CHAPTER 13
## REFLECTIONS
## GOD CREATED MANKIND IN HIS OWN IMAGE
## WHY?

Reflections are the proof that there is an infinitely Powerful Unknown some of us call God, according to our beliefs. This Power is not confined to any particular culture, religion or spiritual tradition. It is beyond words and form; this is why He sends His Messengers to further communicate with us.

Who are the Messengers? All of us including Prophets, religious leaders, family members, co-workers, politicians and even those we encounter casually, like taxi drivers. All messages provoke us with competing thoughts, which are a great challenge to our thought system and may purposely cause frustration. All leading along the same road to unification. As we go on reading, we'll discover again and again, that we were united as a consciousness until we imagined that we split. Then through DNA and the Big Bang, mankind was created as the Image of that Powerful Unknown.

The Powerful Unknown, who is One and the Source of all there is, knows that human beings have been asleep and need to awaken. He knows we are living a dream of awakening, which some of us see as a nightmare. He knows we forget that He is everywhere, therefore in all of us, and in all there is. He is in an invisible form, manifested in Reflections. The Universe is His Reflection.

Another form of reflections on earth is technology, such as computers and cell phones. Indeed, they talk to us. They give us information if we are willing to listen; they can please us or make us miserable. In short, they provoke us. They, too, are being fed by cosmic waves. We think information is downloaded to the machines, when in reality it is being downloaded to us and our reaction uploaded back to our Source. Nothing is lost in the universe. At the moment of the Big Bang, when our thoughts caused us to imagine that we were running away from that Light, all was created as His Image: the image of the Unknown, the One and Only.

What did really happen? It is known that DNA was created in the form of a liquid a few seconds after the explosion started.

The First Image, was the First nucleus and was recognized as Allah, the Initial Creator of crude matter. Therefore, he became known as the God of the Medium he is in, just like there have been other Gods in history. We have read that the Big Bang led to the formation of the world and our existence as crude matter in the form of particles, and that meant separation. But Allah was not alone; Two more Images that followed, were also called Creators. Why? As previously mentioned, the Big Bang explosion was a manifestation of the thought of separation. What was about to be created on earth and beyond, as Reflections of the Unknown (who is ONE), consisted of a countless number of particles that symbolized separation from that Unknown and therefore, could not be just One.

That is why the First Three Images of DNA were also called "Creators," as a Reflection of the Real Creator beyond space and time; only HIM, mentioned as the Unknown, is ONE.

Allah came as One Creator from a State of Oneness. We may also consider him as One. But on earth, he was manifested together with two other Creators. We, too, came from the same State of Oneness. Once on this planet we were created as crude matter, in many shapes and forms, to give us the illusion of separation. Although that Oneness exists within all of us as reflections, it is not manifested in physical form. To discover It, we have to dig deeply into our thoughts. All Three Creators were assigned different names and different missions with the same aim of unification. Let's recall that names are but symbols. It is explained that the Three Creators reflect to the One and vice-versa. This means that all the knowledge human beings receive are a reflection from the One to us. Then, our thoughts/reactions reflect back to the One. Allah participated in the creation of our planet earth and us, in the form of crude matter with the help of The Unknown. It was the Unknown that brought the nuclei to the earth. As it is written, nothing could have come into existence without the sharing of information from The Unknown. This concept of so many Creators may confuse some readers who have difficulty accepting the fact that we develop by going up many ladders of knowledge. These ladders come from the hierarchy of Creators, and from the information accumulated by our many life experiences. This happens until we reach that Unknown.

We may ask: How and where is the information accumulated?
It is explained in detail that recording machines, in a form unknown to us on earth, have been put into effect with the purpose to register our thoughts. This way, Superior Beings, beyond space and time, can follow our development and proceed with their missions accordingly. In the 20$^{th}$ century we were introduced to computers. We had no idea that we, ourselves, are part of a huge and complex computer system with codes and keys to register our cosmic development and awareness. In other words, our thoughts are recorded

beyond space and time, in a form that we can't even imagine while on earth.

Do not be surprised to read that the Three Creators are considered Codes that help us advance gradually because they were the first Nucleic of our existence.

We have heard about city codes, building codes etc. We know they contain rules and regulations. However, we may be astonished to find out that invisible Superior Beings, with the help of cosmic energies, implemented on earth a thought system of development that contains rules and regulations, with codes and keys. They are described and repeated several times, as special and very advanced laws, which were initiated before we existed. They contain the most detailed information of rules and regulations that were put into effect in our planet in the 20th century, although they were brought here by the Three Creators. Such rules and regulations will be hopefully accomplished by all of us by the 30th century. This is why we need the foundations for The Golden Age to be successfully achieved by the end of the 22nd century, and in spite of the difficulties we are facing, we will reach that goal.

Do not be disappointed. Ours is a captivating journey. This means that, in accordance with the form events take in our planet, our Cosmic Journey has taken an indefinite span of time. Only by the 30$^{th}$ century will we enter the Universe of Light, as the unity of our consciousness is hopefully manifested by all of us, sincere human beings, as a Whole. If the unity is not accomplished by that time, there may be adjustments. In other words, we learned slowly and peacefully to share the same thoughts. The question is: What kind of thoughts? Only thoughts of Love and harmony, independent of our backgrounds, are shared. By that time, we have learned to handle the ego, and are able to proceed without thoughts of jealousy, envy, hate, and above all fear.

The reader may wonder why does it take so long? First of all, we have free will, and for this reason, it may take longer than even the Superior Beings expect. Some of the rules and regulations are: Love yourself (take care of yourself, without being selfish), love your enemy, respect nature, and respect humans.

Do these laws sound familiar? Are you ready to go a little further? In the Christian Bible we have the concept of Trinity -The Father, the Son and the Holy Spirit which, after thousands of years still puzzles mankind. Some devotees see God as One who extends to Three Divine Persons. We have the example of Jesus Christ who introduced mankind to Love. Then we were given 2.000 years to experience it.

We forget and even refuse to accept that all of us have been Jews, Moslems, Christians, Buddhists, as well as thieves, murders, loving beings, and more. We have learned a great deal from our millions of years of experiences: this knowledge is stored and blocked in the brain of each individual and is known as the Energy Cord, described in that chapter.

Some of us may imagine that events in our lives are an ongoing repetition, based on our needs from past lives. The ones who can begin to understand life this way, are the lucky ones.

At the moment of the Big Bang, we were created as the Image of that Unknown who is the Source of all there is, including Light.
Why did that happen? The Unknown, that is the Creator, some of us know as God, is Spirit and was not going through the transformation to crude matter like us because Spirit did not cause separation, we did. Here we have perhaps the greatest example of cause and effect, which places God out of the picture.

Therefore, He created us in His Own Image as Reflection and an Extension of Himself, not in material form. That is the reason why Allah came to earth with a mission to participate in the creation of the dimension of crude matter and therefore, material form, in order to help us be transformed back to our rightful state of oneness. As such, he is considered a God by those who love him. He also let us know that without the Power of the Unknown, neither him nor we could exist. This is one of reasons why ours is known as the Age of Truthfulness, and Allah, like all the

Beings, must be respected. This is why it is necessary to repeat that there is no separation.

As it is written in the chapter The Energy Cord, Spirit is not in the body, but it is where our past history is stored. It has been designed this way for while we are on earth. Otherwise if we were aware of our past lives, we would not be able to accomplish our mission the way it is supposed to be accomplished with the help of Cosmic influences and Superior Beings.

Still, we should not close our mind, we should be curious and even interested in digging deeply into the causes of our problems which give us a chance to grow, even if we do not like what is happening.

Those of us who stop searching, are not considered "normal," by Superior Beings. Such individuals can become so narrow-minded that they hurt our progress and delay the development of consciousness. This is the reason why I wrote the following chapter, titled "To be or Not to be normal.".

In the end, it was the Love of the Unknown for us that bought Allah, Jesus and others, to our planet to save us. Again, we forget that they all work as ONE, in a form that it is hard for us to understand, especially because we still see them as separate. It is important to note that neither Allah, nor the Celestial Beings are working now to divulge their religious teachings, but to lead us in a new way to improve our consciousness.

As we advance, even religion will not be necessary, because we discover the potential within all of us. Reflections have been created to manifest the Invisible Power and the Divine Order. It is a form of communication that brings all the information mankind needs, but we need to reflect.

Can we see Light? In other words, can we see truth? Not really; what we see are Its Reflections. Ultimately, reflections are wakeup calls for all of mankind. The Invisible Power is manifested in all there is, and is the source of everything, including us. Even animals reflect the power of the Creator of all Creations to us. What really happened during the Big Bang, was that we were transmuted into matter. Now we've to undo that transformation so that we can go back to our Source.

There are many levels along the way to realize that transformation. All of them are illuminated by an extraordinary energy that has endured many names throughout history; names such as, Sun, God, Goddess, Love, Elohim, Allah, and so forth. Furthermore, religious books have many names attributed to the Creator. It is interesting to note that the word "Allah" was used to symbolize God, long before Islam existed. Although Jews, Arabs, Christians and most religions have accepted that there is only One God, *The KB* and Christianity refer to Creators that are an extension of the ONE, on this planet.

In the end, it is obvious that both religions admit a hierarchy form of learning that brings the necessary experiences for our progress towards unification. The Trinity was especially conceived so that the propagation of Light through reflections would manifest as a Whole with no discrimination, to all there is. In other words, Light communicates to all there is, but the reception of the communication depends on the stage of development of each receiver.  Many of us insist on seeking God without realizing that we are a reflection of Him, and His Reflections are everywhere, including beyond the terrestrial, in all kinds of planets and UFOs.

Seekers are often disappointed when they discover that He lives as a Loving Force in our hearts and that is where we are to search for Him. Others say there is no God. What they want to achieve is impossible, since no one can change what is changeless.  Let's recall that the consequences of the Big Bang are unceasing. Our thoughts are always manufacturing events in our lives, and therefore reflecting them onto the world and back to our Source; it is a demonstration, a showing off, a game.

We are always communicating with the Whole. Thoughts are not lost, and what holds energy and all of us together are the spiral vibrations that contributed to reflections. All things are planned according to our needs. For now, mankind needs reflections. Maybe billions of centuries from now, reflections will be replaced by something else - it all depends on our development. As we have read, although we cannot see the source of Light, we were created in that Image. All things, including ourselves, are mirrors of that image. As such, I am a reflection, and therefore a mirror of you, and you of me.

"He who is without sin among you, let him throw a stone at her first" John 8:7

## CHAPTER 14
## TO BE OR NOT TO BE NORMAL

These days mankind is finding it hard to determine what is normal or not normal. What could possibly have happened to all of us? We have no grounds to be arrogant and say that "I know more than you!" or "This is the only life there is." This means that we are listening only to our own channel which insists in repeating terrestrial thoughts that have dominated our lives for centuries. We are not allowing ourselves to accept the messages from the reflections sent to us from beyond space and time. The truth is that we are always learning. However, most of us are not genuinely interested in discovering the role our hearts and thoughts play in our lives.

We are unaware of our essence, which is the biological constitution of the heart, it is also our values and Spirit, and has consciousness. Then, it carries the knowledge of our origin and our history, even before our existence on this planet. Other cells, besides transmitting energy and representing crude matter (symbol of the ego), also have consciousness.

Therefore, when these two expressions of consciousness join - that is, when the heart and the ego, Light and darkness come together, essence is connected to reasoning, and logic is manifested. This Logic which is the totality of the heart, is celestial. It can connect to the terrestrial logic.

What follows is an episode in my life that illustrates the difference between celestial and terrestrial logic.

For us, 2x2 is 4, which is terrestrial logic. As previously mentioned in the celestial logic, 2x2 may be 12, 14, or more; it all depends on the modes of measuring in other realms which differ from ours. It is based on Micron system, and depends on the frequency of the dimensions we are in; the higher the dimension, the higher the frequency.

When I was in primary school in Europe (in those days I was about age six or seven), I insisted that 2x2 could also be 12, 14, or more. I told that to the teacher. I also tried to investigate! But of course, I was not able to find out the answer until recently. Today, I realize that, like all of us, I was then connected to the celestial, and how beautiful that is!

Fear prevents too many of us from admitting the truth.

In spite of the fact that in order to please the teacher, I went through some discomfort in the process of switching my thoughts, from the Celestial to the terrestrial, I'm grateful that I was capable to recall the correct Celestial information at such a young age. I remember asking, in secret, for help to switch my thoughts. But who was helping me? Furthermore, I did not know that by speaking up, I had become the provoker. I was also not aware, and neither was the teacher, that I was trying to help him open up to new forms of life, while at the same time I was teaching myself a lesson. Of course, the teacher had to react by threatening me with severe punishment if I did not shut up.

My family, on the other hand, still remember to call me "abnormal." I learned to love them for I know I have chosen them to share their life on earth with me. Their attitude was the opposite of the Celestial Beings who are watching us and consider those who follow only the rules of the terrestrial to be not the normal ones.

While we are on earth, the confusion about who or what is normal will become more and more prominent, especially as our thought system advances towards the celestial. Then, we can expect that the reflections we receive become stronger. Now more than ever, I realize how much my devotion to spirituality and metaphysics has helped me clarify my status in society, and in my mind. This is why I have mentioned in another chapter that one of the reasons I am writing *A Cosmic Journey to the Unknown*, is for my own development. In spite of the difference between these two logics (celestial and terrestrial), humans will always be helped in their endeavors to act from the consciousness of their hearts. To do this, all of us need true love, forgiveness, and mutual help. Who helps us? Whether we believe it or not, "Spirit" helps us. For Christians it is the Holy Spirit, as previously mentioned. Since I started my spiritual quest, decades ago, I have been acknowledging how much the Holy Spirit has helped me to adjust to life on earth and to our terrestrial thought system. Now, I understand the importance of reflections in every instance in our lives. This is how we receive communication from the Unknown.

Indeed, in another episode as a very young child, I was aware of the presence of very powerful angels (two, I believe). When the time came for them to leave me, I remember them saying "Goodbye" while I cried and begged them not to go! I was still in my small bed and remember vividly their answer that they should have gone already but "due to the circumstances" they were staying a little longer. I understood their message in a limited way but only recently I understand it fully. I also recall that they mentioned that I could always communicate with them. I remember them frequently. I am grateful to them for saving my life.

Many entities call themselves "spirits," but there is only One, known as the Holy Spirit, that is part of the Essence, and is connected by a thin line to the heart. Therefore, the Holy Spirit does not exist inside our bodies and does not need to evolve, but the essence does, because it is logic and also reasoning, necessary for us to advance while on earth. The Holy Spirit's mission is to reverse our thoughts, by directing them towards our heart whenever necessary, or when we ask for help. Furthermore, as we know, Spirit does not discriminate, meaning that all humans benefit from His direction.

When we accomplish our mission, which is the union of the consciousness of our essence with the cells' logic, we will be able to eliminate all negativities from our thoughts. Only then will we reach perfection, because the cells of the heart are able to communicate with the brain. This may not happen until the Seventh Dimension (we are on the Third Dimension). However, some of us now on earth, may come from there or even from a higher dimension, but choose to be here now in a veiled awareness; that is, as incognitos, in order to help mankind.

We have an enormous task on this planet and beyond. Understanding and accepting our on-going relationship with entities we cannot see is very important. But we are not aware of what we are doing, nor are we aware of the importance of the role of our hearts and thoughts. Furthermore, we don't even try to accept our mission, much less understanding the influence of reflections on us.

It's about time we awaken! And for that reason, we'll have a glimpse of life in other planets in the following chapters.

## CHAPTER 15
## WHERE DO OUR GENIUSES COME FROM?

Have you ever imagined that some planets have people like us? Remember, Stephen Hawking confirmed this concept, then he added that such planets are not common. For that reason, we should not be surprised to read that a planet made of an unknown form of compact metal, has inhabitants like us that wear clothes made out of the same metal after its density is reduced. They do not need air and or light to survive. They too have children without physical contact. Their technology is very advanced and their mission is the surveillance of activities on earth. The purpose of the surveillance is to collect information so that they can help us connect to higher dimensions. If for some reason they cannot communicate with us, they come and get us but we will not be aware. In this case, our magnetic aura and frequency are very important, so that we provide the necessary connections.

This means that they need to research us constantly and are counting on our facilitating their research. This validates what we read in the news and in some magazines about abductions of human beings by unknown sources, or unidentified objects.

Let's first consider that the substance of this planet that exists beyond space and time, in a very compact state, is also a thin metal. If we use the terms of the earth, it seems to have something to do with plutonium a substance that is manufactured by nuclear reactors on earth. But it is not. Interesting enough, we also learn that our planet came from that planet of unknown metal. This does not mean that the substance is the same since it went through transformations. What this means is that our planet was formed from substances which were copies from other galaxies that were transplanted here.

What else have they transplanted to our planet? Geniuses, such as, Edison, Albert Einstein, and Stephen Hawking, who is from the 79$^{th}$ dimension, as we know. If we recall what was written in 3$^{rd}$ chapter, titled "How Do We know We Are Progressing," geniuses like

Leonardo da Vinci, Hendel, Edison, Stephen Hawking were mentioned. These individuals were programmed to be conscious of what they learned, perhaps over the course of millions of years, during many lifetimes and life-cycles on earth. All the information is kept in their Energy Cord. After they are properly trained and guided, they choose to come back to our world. This event has to happen at the appropriate time in our history, so that they adjust their knowledge to meet the actual needs of humanity and teach us accordingly. Intelligence, then, is the union of all our terrestrial thoughts with the celestial, but all of them come from the Beyond.

It should be no surprise to read the following sentence already quoted from Socrates: "I know that I am intelligent, because I know that I know nothing." What happens is that our present needs encounter the information of the very distant past. Where was their past? Certainly, beyond space and time. The events had to be properly coordinated. Can you imagine Edison, Albert Einstein and Hawking coming to earth, say, five hundred years ago with the same teachings? Humanity was not prepared. Only Leonardo da Vinci was able to express future events through his art. He was a precursor of modern science, including Spaceships. What mankind does with teachings, such as religion, scientific, and technological is up to each individual; it can be for better or for worse, as in the case of Albert Einstein. He went through a painful time with the event of the Atomic Bomb, for that was not the purpose of his scientific work. Yet, others benefitted greatly from his work. Here, we can see again the game "duality" plays in our lives.

We are aware that science is speculative: scientists develop new concepts as time goes by.
We are always being helped. Learning never ends. Some of these individuals win the Nobel Prize, others win nothing, still others prefer to stay incognito. Reflect on what is written. Think about Stephen Hawking's life and the impact of his choices, especially taking into consideration his physical health, and his mental state up to his death.

In antiquity some individuals dared to present some of the concepts now accepted, but their proposals disappeared in the whirlpool of fear. Most of the expressions we use in our world do not exist in other worlds. The residents of that metal planet have also learned to manipulate atoms and, one day, we too will do that, so we are told.

Remember Albert Einstein already worked on releasing the atoms. Now, the inhabitants of the metal planet, are ready to send us more geniuses. However, in order for them to do that we need to achieve a more advanced and unified thought system. And for that reason, they hope that we'll use whatever time we have left constructively so that each of us will be able to control our emotions.

The metal from that planet is used in most alien spaceships, and sometime in the future we, on earth, will be able to use it too; it all depends on our progress. Consequently, their message to us is: Don't waste your time with trivialities, so that you can advance and let us help you receive the knowledge of our technology by unifying your consciousness.

## CHAPTER 16
## A PLANET OF GOLD, MUSIC AND COLOR

Imagine a planet of solid gold, flowers and music. Imagine a Planet where the potential of our thoughts are manifested in a way that they command us. From that Planet, you can go anywhere and speak any language without using UFOs, spaceships, airplanes or any means of transportation and/or communication. You will be floating in space, on your own, at a speed faster than we can ever imagine.

Who are the inhabitants of this Planet? First of all, although they don't have a body like us, they are very pleasant, and calm. Their essence is fluid gold which they make by manipulating atoms without damaging them.

Please meditate on this information and note the power of our thoughts. Their breath is like the fragrance of flowers, and food comes from trees. But there are no seeds. If you pick up a piece of fruit, right away another one manifests. Do they have blood? Yes. It comes from rivers, in the form of a drink, which resembles wine. Where do they live? In crystal pyramids and the furniture is pure gold. Other galaxies reflect on them, and they reflect on us. Their clothes are made from the leaves of plants which are fibers that do not wear out. They are a symbol of our potential of a paradise lost, but mankind can regain it once our consciousness develops and we unify. They are able to transmit through thoughts all knowledge they receive to any planet they wish. Therefore, thoughts function at a great speed.

This reminds me of a relationship I once had with a man I was in love with. He was a peaceful man and a hard worker. He was a man of poor means. He had learned how to read and write. I always reminded him to take time off to travel around America and discover its beauty. Unfortunately, he passed away. A few months later, I was home and started to think about him. Unexpectedly, I heard expressions that sounded very familiar:

"I see you all the time. I see America… all over. It is so beautiful. I'm here! You see? You see?"

I had a feeling that he was floating in space, may be above my head, but I did not look. I was surprised and happy to recognize his message and his voice. All happens very fast.

There is an important message to learn from my experience. Several times during our relationship I had a hint of his advanced spiritual development, but I had no idea how advanced he was. I know that when we are with someone even for a minute, whether or not in some type of a relationship, and we realize how calm, gentle, and genuine that person is, we may receive the psychic message that he/she is a very advanced spiritual human being. I am also impressed by the fact, that in just a few months after his death, my friend was in a very advanced dimension. Besides, he was able to communicate with me, which is very difficult for them to achieve once they pass away.

Let me explain why: Such communication has to do with a form of science unknown to us that happen beyond space and time, which we may call physics. All connections have to be perfectly coordinated among all the beings involved; the ones that have passed and the one on earth receiving the message. I was probably sleeping, while the coordination was being done, because I was not aware of anything, including the fact that my permission had to be granted.

Only very powerful and advanced technology beyond the world and beyond our understanding, can accomplish such a task. Without this type of technology, we could not exist. It plays a major role in all events in our planet, and beyond. It helps the Powers beyond space and time accomplish their mission. But that technology does not come from any known Powers but from the Unknown. These are great news, it helps us understand the power of the Creator of all Creations, some of us call God.

# CHAPTER 17
## WHERE IS BERTRAND RUSSELL?

Bertrand Russell was a British Philosopher, 1872-1970. He claims he is a member of the Golden Age, and is now on a UFO watching us. He promises us fascinating days. This event is a reminder that all of us on this planet are preparing to go back without being aware, then we can communicate back to earth in whatever form we choose, depending on our evolvement.

When I was a teenager, in Europe, I read his book "The Conquest of Happiness" in English, and fell in love with him. I wanted him to be my father, but I kept it a secret and never told anybody, not even my father. I read the book many times. I used to sleep with it next to me. Then, I promised myself that I'd go to London to study and I'd look for him. Years later, I arrived in London and the whole sentiment just evaporated: I had conquered happiness, at least for a while. I was surprised and happy, when I read that his journey led him to be on a UFO, and he is promising us happy days.

In the end, his message is that humans are all extraterrestrials, before we come to earth and after. The form that we take depends on our development: in his case his advanced thought system prepared him to be communicating with us from a mechanical form known as UFO. As he advances, he will not need any other form to communicate with us but his thoughts. He will be able to "travel" anywhere he wants at a speed faster that we are not able to measure on earth, just like my friend was doing. The aim of technology is to help us realize our potential to awaken, especially when we have encounters like I just described.

CHAPTER 18
## **TECHNOLOGY**

We have read about the influence of technology in the past and in the future. However, in order to proceed we must consider the reflections happening in the present which in this case have to do with a very advanced technology.

While the Superior Beings collect all our thoughts in diskettes beyond the earth, technology on earth is doing its job collecting our info with computers that have been invented by humans, with the help of those beyond space and time. Therefore, our computers are nothing but distorted copies of what exist beyond planet earth.

Why is this happening now? Both forms of computers, on earth and beyond, have been set up to help mankind advance in the unification of our consciousness and in accordance with our stage of development, even if it causes pain.

The following description of my own experience, may shed some light on this matter. Once, I used my computer for the first time to translate one of my chapters. During the translation, I posed

for a moment. To my great surprise a sentence showed up on the screen written in perfect English;
"You are crazy!" "Hey, this thing is alive," I exclaimed loudly.
From that moment on, I felt a single unified energy like a bowl infused with warm, goldish and very pleasant light, focusing intensively on the right side of my brain. It took a little time to organize, then it was motionless. The event lasted, may be, less than a minute. After this experience, I arrived at the conclusion that Light/Energy could come only from beyond space and time, since human beings do not have the capacity, at least for now, to manipulate them like The Unknown, does.

    In the end, there is only One Source, One computer, One Atom and we already know this but we choose to ignore the truth. For that reason, science is beyond the terrestrial, so is technology: It is this type of technology that comes from beyond space and time, that will, one day, force nations to stop fighting: this is the great dilemma of the 21$^{st}$ century.

Do not be disappointed. Just experience life every second, whether you are aware of dreaming or not. Remember that technology originates from beyond space and time and is always in effect, especially after we dispose of our bodies, as it is written in the next chapter.

CHAPTER 19
## HEAVEN
## REST IN PEACE!

In many cultures, when someone disposes of their bodies the favorite slogan is "Rest in Peace." Obviously, believers and no believers are aware that we don't just disappear. For some individuals this is very comfortable, imagining that one day they will meet again, while for others their egos convince them to think differently; out of sight, out of mind, good riddance. As you read this chapter, please consider that I get the information from very reliable sources, which I respect and accept. Most important, I am not writing fiction and I did not write The Knowledge Book.

Please keep in mind that mankind's only problem is our thought of separation. The present chapter, is another example of this truth. We discover that what we are learning at present, in our 3rd dimension, our world, leads to another and to another until they are replaced by some other thought system may be millions of years, or centuries from now. This confirms what was already written: all is entangled.

Dimensions, then, are used as evolution scales. As we evolve, all the info is saved and transferred to a higher dimension.

Let's proceed to inquire about some of the steps necessary to reach the 4$^{th}$ Dimension which we call Heaven, and then go on to the others.

How do we earn the right to enter Heaven? In principle, it is not our choice to enter Heaven; it is a must so that humanity proceeds to evolve. But to earn the right to enter heaven is not easy. Our evolution starts between the 3$^{rd}$ and the 4$^{th}$ Dimension and there are 3 steps; Earthly Cognition, Heavenly Cognition, Universal Cognition which Encompasses the Whole. All of them contain the knowledge necessary to advance.

<u>First Step of our Evolution</u>: The Earthly Cognition, happens in our world (3$^{rd}$ Dimension). It deals with religion. It has several levels. We enter heaven when we successfully accomplish them all. What happens after death? First, we are levitating in an unconscious state. Is the reader surprised? Are we aware that while on earth, too often we realize or

someone tells us that we are not conscious? How can we be conscious if we are dreaming?

Meditate on this truth: most of the time, while on earth, we are not really aware of what we are doing and even why. Too many times, we are not aware of what we are saying, either.

Then, as we depart from this world after attaining so much misleading information, it must be confusing and hard to be aware of the truth: especially when we recognize that our thoughts go on. We hope to continue in our state of unconsciousness: imagining that we can just fall asleep, and we never have to think about anything, and never have to take any responsibility either, not even awakening. We, certainly, can expect a great surprise. While on earth, our education does not prepare most of us to distinguish between what is true and what is false. That is why we need religious books but only for a short time. Why? There will be a time when our development is such that we realize the great power within us, and finally, we awaken. It should be no surprise to find out at the moment of death that our

thoughts go on and so does life.
Unfortunately, the opposite may happen.
Who is Thinking? Obviously, our brain never stops.

It must be shocking to realize that with or without a brain, we can still think. Life and death are full of surprises.
When we pass away, we'll be facing many events in our lives with all the figures in it, and even compare with past lives, in tremendous awe.
There will be an instant when we realize how easy it was to destroy while on planet earth, whereas it is difficult to build once we pass away.
We may have to make amends. We may need to atone. Logic and reason play a major role in our awakening. In order to help us in this difficult stage, we have Beings beyond space and time, always ready to make it easier for us. It must be obvious that for some of us it is easier to go through this level, while for others, such as those who commit suicide, or murder, it is very difficult; it delays their development, while some advance to higher dimensions, others have to stay behind floating in their unconscious state and waiting their turn.

A lot has been written by many individuals about the state of Heaven/Hell. The image I have of this state, is Dante's Inferno, part of his Divine Comedy, which describes our hard journey until we reach Paradise. Dante was an Italian poet born 1265AD.

After our long journey, which for some is very difficult, we start to become aware and receive Light. Since Light conveys knowledge, we become conscious, and cognizance follows. After that there are several stages of worship which end with us being conscious of the need to worship through the heart.

Second Step of our evolution: Heavenly Cognition, happens in the $4^{th}$ Dimension: Heaven. It functions together with $3^{rd}$ Dimension. Now, we are beginning to see how there is no separation, everything is really entangled and the time we need to disentangle is up to all of us. As a matter of fact, we do not complete our evolution until we reach more dimensions. Our evolution advances gradually. Heavenly cognition also has several levels, and a different type of knowledge is introduced.

First is the level of accomplishment. If you need help, the Beings beyond space and time will help you, as described in the chapter titled "Twin Universe: A Ghost." The other levels are for instance, Divine connections which are given to you.

Finally, you are introduced to a Technological Dimension, which has to do with space and you travel in UFOs. Like this you are now facing the Truths: Our thoughts never end.

And Yes, UFOs exist. I have mentioned Bertrand Russell in another chapter, a British philosopher who lived last century and introduced himself to Mevlana while she was taking notes. He claims he is in a UFO helping us. His message to us is that all of us are extraterrestrials before we come to earth and after we leave the earth. And the fact that the acceptance of this knowledge is missing in our education, is very damaging to humanity.

The First Evolution (earthly) ended just before Heaven, and before the introduction of technology. Does mankind have any idea of the tremendous influence of technology and the games we all like to play?

What happened to the terrestrial body we are leaving behind? We are told that in spite of being in the $4^{th}$ dimension, we still have our biological body (earthly body) but with the following difference: We have another body waiting for us: It consists of rays of Light which are infused in our earthly body. Then, our body looks more like a great light than just crude matter. We see this in movies about ghosts, as mentioned in another chapter.

What happens then? We look much younger. This information reminds me of another event in my life that I have written about many times before. The husband of one of our friends passed away. My parents and I visited the family after the funeral. To our great surprise, we found out that a few seconds after his death, he completed change from looking a senior to looking like a teenager. This meant that he had completed his evolution.

At the end of this dimension, (Heaven, $4^{th}$ Dimension) if we succeeded, we start to contact the $5^{th}$

Dimension. All our cells are transported from one dimension to another.
First, cells have to be purified, that is, infused with rays of Light, as we know. Then, they also become incombustible. In order for us to go through this transformation, we need to rest again, so we go to sleep. All of this happens still in the 4th Dimension. Our cells go through a great transformation.

They start to freeze. Then, we develop special cells which are very powerful and will help us exist in other dimensions in whatever shape and form we choose. We will start to sense the effects of this event in our brains, and perhaps be surprised to find out that we are always following rules and regulations. As our thoughts intensify, we use logic and reason. Let's remember that in spite of the fact that we left the earth, we still are able to think.

Now, that we have reached Heaven, that we have been introduced to Space, that we have travelled in UFOs, that we are purified, and are incombustible, that we have developed very powerful brain cells, what else do we have to do to reach perfection? A lot more.

We have to go through the Third Step of our Evolution: Cognition that encompasses the Whole. It is Universal. It means all cosmoses, and all the galaxies and happens in the Fifth Dimension. The mission of this dimension is to prepare us to higher dimensions where our cells become so advanced that we go even further. In this $5^{th}$ Dimension, we are prepared to enter dimension of immortality by going to very advanced areas, where the need for religion is no longer in effect. The Heavenly Beings presume that we have learned enough to enter other plans. We can transport ourselves to many planets and become embodied there. Then, we may be able to reach Omega, and from there advance to many more dimensions.

Although for many centuries we were told Omega is Heaven, and all our troubles end there, now we know that our cosmic journey after the $4^{th}$ Dimension, goes on and on and Omega supervises us. As we can see, our evolution is endless: Thinking makes it so.

Let's remember that resting in peace depends on us!

In this sense, what is the role of Allah's mission?

## CHAPTER 20
## WHO IS THE ALLAH IN *THE KOWLEDGE BOOK*?

It is written in Genesis that having created the heavens, the earth, the sea, herbs and animals God saw that "It was good." Then He created Adam and Eve and told them what to do in order to live in paradise, but they did not follow His advice. As a result of their behavior, all hell broke loose.

While the Bible does not give dates of Creations, now we are able to read about what happened before the Creation of Adam and Eve and what will happen in the future, whether humanity survives or not.

All events have been carefully prepared and will continue to evolve under the guidance of Invisible and Powerful Celestial Beings. This does not diminish the value of the Creation of Adam and Eve, as described in the Bible: it is the opposite, it reminds humanity of the Infinite Power of the Creator.

Many of us wonder how and why a Loving Creator, mentioned as The Unknown, who is beyond matter, and even words, created us in the form of crude matter? This is a question that mankind has not been able to solve until now. As previously described, in the Chapter titled Reflections, it was not The Unknown that caused our problems. We were the ones that imagined the split in our consciousness and created the cause and the effect. Therefore, blaming The Unknown is out of the picture.

As we proceed, we learn in detail, again and again, that The Unknown gave some of His Power to Allah who then participated with other Creators, in the formation of crude matter.

All Creators came to earth, like all of us, in order to help humanity. This means that, on earth, there is a hierarchy of Creators but none could exist without the unification of the Power of the Unknown with Allah's. This is the truth. It is one of the reasons why our Age is considered the Age of Truthfulness.

Let's not forget that the word Allah, is a Symbol of the Unknown Power. This does not diminish the love people have for Allah, and for all the other Powers. What this shows is that there is no separation among all of Creation.

Humanity has forgotten that we imagine we have separated from that Eternal Unity that exists within all of us. This is why we need to awaken. As a result of our imagination, our consciousness, which was a unified whole, seems to split; now we must recover it. This is the reason why our thought of separation is humanity's only problem: and we must keep this sentence in mind, so that we stop blaming, Allah, God, The Unknown, family members, certain groups and organizations for our misunderstandings.

It is Allah's mission together with Superior Beings like Jesus Christ, Moses, Mohammed, to lead us to accomplish our return without force, that is, our awakening.

It is written that the Big Bang, known as the first great explosion, is a symbol of the burst of our consciousness from unity to complete disaster. This event led to duality in our thought system: we went from True-Love to false love, from spirit to matter and so the ego became active. Then, we forgot everything. As a consequence of our forgetfulness, the pain of separation started, as well as the necessity to return

to a unified consciousness. For this reason, Allah and all of us before we were created in the form of crude matter, manifested on earth at the Big Bang. This is to remind us that we are all on the same boat, navigating with an Invisible Captain. Now, perhaps more than ever, mankind is struggling to accomplish this return, and go beyond the Beyond.
We must be aware that we are running out of time. Therefore, the reader must let go of preconceptions, and try and read with an open mind, a mind without fear.

    In the 20th century, we were surprised by the publication in Turkey, of *The KB*, which had apparently been prepared for an indefinite period of time, in accordance with our needs. It took 12 years for Mevlana to handwrite it. She receives energies from many dimensions.

    As previously mentioned, in Christianity, the Three Powers are a reflection of the Trinity: Father, Son and Holy Spirit, and a symbol of the oneness created and sustained by a Power unknown to all of us. In this way, the human race, as it exists on this planet, was manifested. Crude matter could not have simply "happened" without the power of that Unknown that no one knows anything about—other than that It IS.

It was that Unknown Power that fed the necessary information to form all there is, including the nucleus, nucleic world, and DNA. Allah, being the first nucleus formed at the Big Bang, is considered a symbol of that Power. Humanity is now informed, for the first time, that it does not matter what planets, galaxies, or universes we are in, hierarchies are always in progress, until we get to the Unknown. In this sense, learning is unending. On the other hand, we know we are more than crude matter: our thoughts take us beyond the body, beyond the physical, beyond what we can see. For this reason, each human is seen as a consciousness, not as a body. Furthermore, it was a very Powerful Intelligence that created fire, Light and sound, and all knowledge comes from there. In spite of the fact that The Celestial Beings that participate in *The KB* do not know what this Power is, they consider it to be a Natural Energy, which they call Allah. It is explained that Natural Energy is from unknown sources.

It is important to understand that Allah, during most of this process, is not in physical form; He is a dimension that shows us many steps, also known as rungs on ladders, for us to achieve salvation far beyond Omega. He is also a universal brain and an extraordinary computer, beyond our imagining. In addition, he is a great creative power which is a reflection of the Invisible Intelligence. He clarifies some aspects of the Koran and helps people from all religions look at themselves in a different light. Yes, go ahead and wash your body, but do not forget to wash away your ego. It is further written that we should not fear dogma or worship figures from any religion but take bits of their wisdom and experience them. The moment we say or think, that "I am better than you," we are securing our place in a box called conditioning, sealed shut by pride. We prevent ourselves from developing if we do not break free of that box and open our spiritual eyes to new horizons. We are therefore asked to eliminate especially our religious conditionings so that we can help ourselves and mankind. This process has to be accelerated because we are running out of time.

It is also written that Islam means Authentic Human Beings, and that is achieved when the brain unites with the heart. Then our intellect, logic and awareness play a major role in our achievement. It is Allah's last hope, together with all Celestial Beings, that humanity as a Whole will succeed in this endeavor, without violence. This does not mean that we'll have to become Islam, or to accept the Moslem religion, so it is written in *The Text*.

The Celestial Beings are reformers and peaceful revolutionaries. Like us, most of them have been on earth.

It is mentioned that we cannot achieve peace of mind by force.

However, as we continue reading, we get the impression that it is some kind of brainwashing. Even if we consider it so, we must realize that its thought system is not imposed on us by any outside force but comes of our own volition. Our free will plays a major role in the way we think and act. We have choices. Some readers wonder if *The KB* is the focus of a cult. First of all, a cult has to have a leader and they have no leader. Besides, as previously mentioned, no one under the age of 18 is allowed. Mevlana, the scriber, lives in Turkey. She considers herself a Missionary not a psychic. She has responsibilities while she is on earth and gets all the information from The Superior Beings beyond space and time. Allah Himself is not with us now. He is in a more advanced dimension, known as "Beta Nova" which is still being created. He is waiting for us to join him in the future. Beta Nova is described as a planet where we, humans, will go and create a new civilization. He informed mankind that he will show up on earth, and stay for a short while, when we are ready, and when our thought system is completely changed.

It is mentioned that in our present system, known as the $4^{th}$ Plan of Allah, which started in the year 2000, those who commit murder are not accepted. This is a reminder of what is written in the chapter titled Heaven and the information about levitating in an unconscious state in an area where whose who commit suicide and or murder are waiting for permission to proceed to higher and more advanced dimensions. That permission is delayed because others that are more advanced will go ahead in their journey to higher dimensions, at a faster speed. Moreover, the concept of destroying those Muslims who do not believe, as described in The Koran, may imply the use of force. Like all religious books, The Koran was written hundreds of years ago when, according to Allah, battles were necessary, but in accordance with what is written, now there is no more need for wars.

    This concept can also be a reminder to mankind to learn to peacefully handle the ego, which causes so much pain and lack of faith in our potential to create and to love. In the chapter about the devil, we've the example of how Jesus answered the devil's temptation. Our way to approach the ego must be accomplished harmoniously by each of us, without fear and independent of any religion. It cannot be removed by force.

In the end, we must have faith; but, we must not become obsessed with it. This is the reason for the on-going cycles of life. Obsessions may lead to chaos and even violence. We have a great job ahead. We have to learn to handle the ego patiently and see through it so that our lack of True-Love is corrected. We have to learn to conquer ourselves peacefully because we have implanted within ourselves so much fear that, too often, we've allowed the ego to take charge of our existence.

Buddha was right in his interpretation of true conquest:

"One may conquer in battle
A thousand times, a thousand men,
Yet he is the best of conquerors,
Who conquers himself."

*The KB* is not a book about Allah and it is not a political book: It is a book that prepares us for the future. It is a guide for all of us to understand life in this world and beyond; it is science and psychology. Its teachings are very similar to Madame Blavatsky's, co-founder of a philosophy known as Theosophy, established in America in 1875. It is based on ancient wisdom. It teaches that all things are part of a whole, that real religion is the truth, and that we can know God through science.

Let's also recall that Egypt participated in the formation of the alphabet which started with the hieroglyph. Those who had awaken their consciousness were able to receive the knowledge necessary to invent calligraphy and even printing machines. As such, libraries were created, including a great library in Alexandria which was destroyed by a fire in the $3^{rd}$ century BC. Why a fire? It is written that humanity was not ready to accept such knowledge, and their ego could create chaos. Does this sound familiar?

This event was a prelude to the birth of the Photon Technique, mentioned in previous chapters, which has so much influence in the way our brain reacts to the letters as we read *The Text.* And if we succeed, we'll advance to become truthful humans at a faster rate than ever. Besides, *The KB* is not about religion, yet it encompasses all religions because, as we have read, all things are one inside the other and The

Unknown, is an Eternal Power beyond all Worlds. All things include thoughts that exist on earth and in other planets, worlds, universes, that represent the past; They are twins.

In addition, humanity is informed, for the first time, that Islam means Sincere Human Being, which is achieved when the brain unites with the heart, after we go up many ladders. This lack of understanding causes chaos in the Muslim society, and in all societies. Indeed, all of us have to go up many ladders in order to unite. In the meantime, we are receiving positive energies of the more advanced plans through frequencies that analyze our thoughts and measure vibrations, which have to do with our emotions. This is what makes it a healing book. This is the authors' way to watch and see if our thoughts are bounded to the earth, or if we can go beyond the terrestrial. When we are ready, they start to help us in a way that we are not aware of. Indeed, we are never alone: there is a silent work always in progress within us, monitoring and measuring. The silent work continues throughout our lives past,

present, and future, whether we believe it or not. In the meantime, since they know our whole history, it is possible for them to direct events throughout the world. The system is set up this way in order to prepare us for a better future and show us that our only power is the power of Thought. Hopefully, we will accomplish what is written in the Bible, Mathew 6:10:
"Your Kingdom come.
Your Will be done, on earth as it is in heaven."

One day we will be living in harmony with friends and even enemies. This is the aim of the New Golden Age we will create. Only after reaching that age we advance to beyond The Beyond - that is, to the Age of Light, beyond levels of learning, hierarchies, and fallacies.
Do not be intimidated by this information; it will take centuries for mankind, as a Whole, to realize such a state in its thought system, a state that will be beyond errors in thinking, beyond what we call government, and beyond what we know as learning: a state of our unified consciousness.

Each letter in *The Text* is charged with an extraordinary energy in accordance with the potential of each individual. We take in what we are conscious of at any given moment. As we go on reading, we'll reach higher and higher frequencies as our thoughts go beyond the terrestrial. And this is the key that opens us to new dimensions. Then we will transcend earthly consciousness and be completely transformed, from caterpillar to butterfly and beyond.

Our Guides' mission, is to oversee a process that leads mankind to perfection. Their intention is that we learn to handle our emotions and manage the ego with the help of the technique already described, but still unknown to us. This is a Power that is beyond energy. We can gain this Power by working towards the unification of our consciousness. As we have read, this Power activates humanity beyond its terrestrial thoughts and consists of a Photon at a speed that we have yet to experience. This technique, which acts like a cyclone, empowers our brain so that we unite everyone not only in this world, but in many others that we are not yet conscious of. Eventually, all of us will reach our salvation and the Beyond.

As we develop, we are going to embrace all of humanity, and love all that there is with True-Love, which is the rocket that propels us to go beyond our terrestrial thoughts towards the universal. We must consider others, not just ourselves. We must respect others. At the same time, we must love ourselves, and take care of our mental and physical health. We must also be at peace with ourselves and understand that True-Love exists in all of us. True-Love is the understanding and the acceptance of what we really are, and our need to ask forgiveness of ourselves and others. True-Love is the wish and the intention to embrace all there is, not just the human, but all other forms, expecting nothing in return. True-Love is being conscious of the existence of that "Particle" within all forms, including us, that unites all there is.

Often, in our desperate need to remember, we give up hope and understanding of True-Love. And for that reason, we may even become barbarians.

It is the height of arrogance to imagine we are alone. Beings from other planets are constantly trying to contact us, but our capacities are very limited for the time being. In the summer of 2014, astronomers received, over a period of weeks, three intense signals through cosmic rays. They are still trying to find out where they come from and what they might mean. Our potential to evolve is such that, in spite of our slow progress, we are creating the foundations for the (New) Golden Age, which leads mankind to proceed to the Age of Light. We already know that the basic preparation takes three centuries, from the $20^{th}$ through the $22^{nd}$. This information, helps us understand what is written in the $2^{nd}$ chapter about our need for "a push" at the beginning of the $20^{th}$ century. In the meantime, by end of the next century ($22^{nd}$), our thoughts will begin to materialize both inwardly and outwardly. We may start to rule our own lives since the means of production will change and hopefully, we will no longer depend so much on others for our survival.

It is written that we have already achieved some progress, by accepting

only One God, The Unknown, as the Creator of All Creations, who gave power to Allah and to all of us in order to proceed with our mission on earth.
In the meantime, we have an enormous task ahead of us, as we gradually learn to be at peace so that there will be no more wars, within us and outside of us. Suffering helps us understand life and is necessary for us to evolve. We can learn from suffering and sometimes we can alleviate it. Allah's peaceful mission will be accomplished when his sincerity is accepted by people of all religions and of no religion.

    In the end, a big question arises: Who rules us?

CHAPTER 21

# ARE MEN FIT TO RULE MEN?

Plato, who lived about 400 years before Christ, wrote in the *Book of Laws*, that "men are not fit to rule men." It meant that at least 400 years before Christ, humans did not have the necessary brainpower to rule themselves, much less to rule others. This assertion is true still to this day. Therefore, as always, we need the participation of Invisible Superior Beings, who work as One, to help us. Those of us who think that there is too much bureaucracy on this planet, will be surprised to read that only very powerful Invisible Beings, beyond our imagination, can handle the hierarchies within this vast construction, under a Divine Plan. Some, or maybe all of these Beings, have been on earth. Then, they choose to become channels in order to relay the information to us.

It is interesting to recognize names like Bertrand Russell, and also Greek mythological figures like Poseidon (sea god), and playwriters like Sophocles, but we have to go beyond the myth. Therefore, watch out! We are always being watched, observed and seen for what we are by more entities than we can imagine. They ask us to do the same to ourselves. In addition, we are informed that some galaxies do not want Allah, but he does his best to keep them away. This new information leads us to believe that there is controversy beyond the earth. In the future, during this learning process, Allah will show up in physical form like us. He will rule temporally over the world.

As already described, this will be accomplished not by force, but with the help of mankind's advanced thought system and brain development, strengthening willpower.

Of course, Allah's desires are not new; humanity has always wished to be free of wars and at peace. These ideas were advanced on our planet, especially during last century, by the "New Age" movement. However, what is new is the admission that a benevolent Allah, who participated in the formation of crude matter, and making the Laws effective, is the ruler of this dimension we call "world." Such Laws promote our levels of learning and our resulting progress. He also asks for our cooperation to save us. The truth is that all of us are trapped here, in our 3$^{rd}$ dimension, with a specific mission to be accomplished and we need to get out. We need to go beyond dimensions. Also new is the detailed and complex scientific information relating to events in the past, in the present, and in the future.

We are being warned about the Truths that will shape up our future. Some of the events are confirmed by scientists, especially astrologers. For instance, why are so many people depressed right now, and why are there so many mental health problems? It is explained that they are created by energies that come from far beyond space and time, already mentioned as Cosmic. These energies form strong cosmic waves to provoke us and cosmic currents to give us knowledge.
The information is difficult for many of us to handle due to our ego's responses of guilt, fear, anger, and other resistance that we have not yet learned to face. This tremendous task is accomplished by the Spirit and requires our faith. We can rest assured that Spirit does not

discriminate. If we ask, all of us will get help whether Muslims, Christians, secularists, atheists and so forth. There are also many references to provocations at all levels, including family, social and professional. We've had glimpses of the meaning of provocations in other chapters. The aim of these provocations is to stimulate our thoughts and feelings, while our Celestial Beings observe us and study our progress, as well as our form of handling conflicts, which is based on separation.

For that reason, we may now understand that participation in provocations is the mission of everyone on earth. In other words, we provoke each other. We may imagine that Karma, (cause and effect) are the reasons for our dilemmas. But we must not become involved in any discussions. It is better to proceed and see our inner battles differently. It is better to ask how can we handle the situation right now. Don't be surprised when you encounter all kinds of characters in your daily affairs. They may be good or bad, or neither, but they are scheduled to be given to you at the appropriate time in your life. Do not fear:

look them in the eye and, remind yourself that Love is always the answer. Remember that you too provoke others.

In the end, what we are going through is an intense transition from terrestrial thoughts to universal and beyond. This can only be achieved with True-Love.

No government on earth has the ability to succeed in this environment without the help of Superior Invisible Beings. Depressions are also exacerbated and sometimes even caused by atomic explosions underground plus the fact that we are still receiving the consequences of the Big Bang in the form of shock waves. Many fish and even dolphins have died of cerebral shock from those vibrations as they contact the water. We humans suffer too as long as our consciousness is split.

It is emphasized that if you are a Christian Jesus is your guide: and He engrafted us with True-Love. If you are a Muslim, Mohammed is your guide and He engrafted us with knowledge just as Moses did. However, quite often one may get the wrong impression that some of the Celestial Beings are trying to dissolve our idea of a Creator. They claim our knowledge is partial and very limited and so we must open up to new horizons. They also claim that the real purpose is not to do away with our idea of a Creator, whatever concept we may have of Him, but to help mankind reach Him. Eventually we will understand that we can create but only with His help and therefore, participation.

The conclusion is that humans are not fit to rule themselves, much less to rule others. Our only power is the force of will necessary to adjust our thoughts to ideas beyond the terrestrial.

It is also written in Revelation 1:8: "I am the Alpha and the Omega, "the Beginning and the End," says the Lord…"

There are important messages in this passage that can help us understand the information we are trying to convey. The Bible was written thousands of years ago when atoms, genes, cell division, the speed of Light, UFOs etc., were unknown. The Dimension of Alpha, (which by the way is the Dimension in which *The KB* was written) was understood as the beginning of life and Omega the end. Consequently, the dimension of Omega meant that after death we go to heaven; that is, if we behaved. There is, however, another surprise, as previously written: We have read that we are in heaven. If we don't agree, it is up to us to examine our consciousness, and rediscover the truth, that is, the fact that we never left.

We know that there are references in the Bible pointing to the fact that there is more than one Heaven. But at that time in human history, mankind was not prepared to understand Omega and even go beyond it. Only now due to advances in technology and also in our cognition, we are ready to progress and accept the knowledge of many other dimensions, some of which the details of their formation and existence remain unknown.

As previously mentioned, Omega is not the end but the continuation of our journey to reach many heavens, meaning many worlds and galaxies, which finally lead us to perfection. As described in the chapter titled "Heaven," after we die (that is, after we dispose of our physical bodies), life goes on in different forms and Omega continues to supervise us. Our brain is always active. Either through reincarnations or not, our thoughts continue until we reach the Beyond, of the Beyond. Eventually, we realize that our major problem is the erroneous thought of separation from that great unity: The One Atom, The Light, The Unknown that implanted His seed in all of us and has been rejected because of fear and our lack of faith. Thus, we do not look into our hearts.

We are aware that our planet is of the Third Dimension (length, width, height). According to Albert Einstein, Time is the fourth dimension which we know as Heaven: this is to remind us it is time to awaken.

There are billions of dimensions, that is, worlds and galaxies; and as we have read some without air, others without light. Some of their inhabitants are interested in our development, in spite of the fact that they see us as ants. Others are interested in our feeling and expression of love while we believe we need their technology. The aim of technology is to help us reach God through science. This is why computers were created. Still, we are not ready to utilize the technology of other dimensions. Our thought system has to be more advanced, otherwise we could cause still more chaos in the world. It is true that as they say, they can destroy us at the touch of a button. It is also interesting that Stephen Hawking, the well-known theoretical physicist, announced in September 2014 that the God Particle, which had been recently discovered by scientists at the Cern laboratory in Switzerland, could wipe out the universe.

There is enough information to revolutionize the educational system in every nation on earth, but they don't want to divulge it, because the more we advance, the less power our leaders will have. The whole world is therefore hostage to the so-called elites, who refuse to open the doors to the truth. They even provoked scientists like Stephen Hawking.

Thanks to some Nasa scientists, it became recently known, that proof of the existence of life in other planets already exists however, it must be kept secret. That information would boost the advancement of mankind in all aspects of life.

In the meantime, we are being kept in darkness, so that we do not see the "Light." Too many of us refuse to accept the work done by NASA and the reports from Brookings Institution, although they are not telling us all they know.
Are we ready to face such a dramatic change in history? For example, if we see what looks like a small green man strolling along Main Avenue, do we say to ourselves: "Oh! It is one of those foreigners! I'll cross over to the other side of the street!"

For mankind to achieve a new understanding of all aspects of life on earth and beyond, books need to be revised, teachers have to be trained anew. Students must be told the truth at a very young age. But, to do this, Love is necessary. The truth is simple, the words we use make it difficult.
There is the invention of the Infinite Machine, a computer known as D-Wave which has come on the market for about $10 Million. There is a great deal of

secrecy surrounding it. It is supposed to help mankind in every area of life, including discovering the likelihood of having cancer before it happens. This company was founded by private entrepreneurs, and it looks as if the business is picking up. In addition, a Japanese company that builds space elevators promises that by 2050 we can travel to the moon at a much cheaper rate than that offered by spacecraft. Japan is also building an underwater village for humans: We've yet to explore the importance of this event.

As far as UFOs are concerned, we are informed that they are shutting down nuclear missiles. The question is, which ones and where? Recently, the sixth man that walked on the moon, Apollo 14, astronaut Edgar Mitchell has provided information based on his experience, as well as other astronauts. It seems that extraterrestrials have been attempting to keep peace on earth by disrupting our weapons. Some claim that their missiles have been disabled by UFOs. In America, there is an area known as Area 51 where classified military research of unidentified aircraft has been secretly in progress for a long time. In the meantime, to our great surprise, China just announced their moon landing on the far side/dark side of the moon, where neither Americans nor Russians have ever landed. The advantage of this event is that they can bring information to the earth: that is, if they want to share such information with the world.

In the end, who rules us? It is easier for us to imagine that we are ruled by the bureaucracy presently on the earth. Yet, with some openness on our part, we know deep down that a Powerful Unknown, and Invisible Forces, working as One, are the Ultimate Rulers. They include Allah, Jesus Christ and all the Powers already mentioned. Nevertheless, Allah tells us that his mission on earth is temporary and that his power comes from the Beyond, which is true of all of us.

We definitely need Superior Invisible Beings to guide us, so that all of us can transcend, knowing that there are others to help us.

After that mass transformation, we will become aware that the power to create lies within ourselves. Our thoughts will lead us beyond the present system so that we can recover our consciousness and reunify. We'll be able to accept the possibility that we have existed before in other galaxies and beyond galaxies. Then, we'll go back there again and again until we awaken. In principle all of us are extraterrestrials who have chosen to be temporarily in flesh and bones in order to accomplish a mission perfectly designed for us to unify.

At some point, we will understand that we are fit to rule ourselves without force.

## CHAPTER 22

## A *PRIORI* – WE EXISTED BEFORE

Some of the other worlds have people similar to us in appearance who live harmonious and peaceful lives, although they have a different style of what we may call civilization. We forget that we too come from beyond space and time and are preparing to go back. Why are we not yet able to live harmoniously on this planet? As previously mentioned, we must understand that planet earth was set up as a school: we are here to learn our lessons and, above all, to pass exams.

Reincarnation plays a major role in our development, yet it does not seem to exist in other galaxies in the form that we know on earth. We know that this planet was specifically designed for us to handle reincarnation.

It is written that our planet was created close to our origin which was the Second Universe and the Big Bang. As such, our potential to create is huge. Here is where the first particles from the Big Bang were formed. So, our energy is higher and more potent than other planets. While we are on this planet, we are used for research and experiment not only for our own benefit, but also for others beyond space and time that need to understand love and the importance of consciousness.

While we are on earth, cause and effect, which we too often ignore, rule our lives. We are very important for the evolution of all dimensions because of our varied levels of learning, and also our accomplishments. For that reason, we must appreciate our mission. In order to succeed, we need patience among other values. All the information is written in a way to stimulate our thought system. This is the form the Celestial Beings can check on our progress: Are we able to discern what is true and what is false? Of course, learning always requires a certain discipline, and respect on the part of all of us.

The Powerful Beings beyond space and time, are aware that all knowledge is based on a *priori* knowledge, which means that it happened or was made before and without examination, because we did not exist as humans at the time it was created. This also means that they are aware of the details of our past lives and future needs while we, on earth, are not. This idea opens our eyes to the fact that all we are doing is repeating over and over again events that happened even before our many life cycles on earth, but we are not allowed to remember.

It is necessary to repeat events that we have misunderstood, or were not ready to accept and for that reason, we have not been able to correct our thoughts.
It is clear from reading The Text that although they don't mention the term A *Priori*, such knowledge comes from reasoning and is based on self-evident truths.

It is also written that in accordance with our potential all of us are on different missions. We can read *The Text,* over and over again, even in the most remote areas of the world, by ourselves and accomplish a mission not only by reading but also by following its principles, which include love and respect for nature and humans, among others. It is further recommended that we be gregarious and socialize, so that our thoughts reflect on other beings, and vice versa. For example, we may come out of a meeting or, a short conversation with someone very pleased because everyone agreed or, very depressed because of contradictions and conflicts. Such encounters, as expressed in the chapter on Reflections, are necessary for mankind to awaken. It is also written that depending on our progress, our thoughts start to reflect on 1000 individuals present anywhere with the same coordinate, meaning with the same thoughts of love and harmony.

This information gives us a chance to understand how Moses, Jesus Christ, Buddha, Mohammed and others, had so many followers at a time without the technology we have today. It all had to do with Reflections. In this sense, all of the Beings mentioned above, had the same thoughts about unity, peace, and love which then reflected straight to the heart of many individuals who were ready to receive their message, independent of the fact of their location. In the end, it is clear that it is not a machine, like a visible computer, that provides us with knowledge, but a type of technology that has always existed beyond space and time, and beyond what our eyes can see.

This is the technology that gives us the cosmic energies necessary for us to evolve. Whether we believe it or not, we are always preparing our future for the benefit of mankind, even when our actions seem to be inhuman. The truth is that we are not aware that we are following the law of cause and effect as already explained, which in our dimension requires reincarnation, a concept that half of the world's religions and people do not accept.

Because we are not aware of the details of our past lives, we tend to repeat the same mistakes, over and over again. We do not want to forgive. We do not love ourselves. In other words, we are sadists and masochists; many humans get pleasure from being hurt and hurting others. This becomes even more difficult for mankind to handle if we do not accept the idea of reincarnation. This is the way the human dynamic has been set up and as we know, it cannot be changed. In *The Text* there are also references to the dimension of Atlanta and how much it influenced our formation and development before the existence of our planet, this will be presented in others chapters.

One of the proofs, or at least suggestions, of the existence of a very advanced civilization (about 2 billion years ago) is in the Republic of Gabon, in Africa. It consists of nuclear reactors several kilometers long, discovered in the Oklo mine.

Some scientists have tried to explain the way these reactors could have been formed, but they cannot prove it. Other scientists are not able to discover their origin, nor the details of their formation. They conclude only that these reactors consist of Uranium ore, and for that reason, classify them as a "natural reactor." Many also wonder if it is possible that a civilization more advanced than ours could ever have existed.

We'll read about Atlanta Dimension and even Atlantis, in other chapters. We are aware that ours is a planet of symbols and reflections: we are urged to wake up. But we need mass awakening because, as we know, all of us are on the same boat. This does not mean that we have to convert to any religion. It is, in fact, just the opposite. One day we'll go beyond religion-- that is, when we are ready to embrace and understand the Power of that Unity that is our essential being. We, too, are symbols: We are figures on a stage acting out a dream of separation from our True Loving Creator of All Creations: a dream of our split consciousness that we are in the process of reuniting. Our reality is somewhere else; it exists but not in what we see on earth. Therefore, the universe is but a reflection of that Reality. And, we are reflections of our previous existences.

CHAPTER 23

## PROTOTYPES AND REINCARNATION

It is written in John 14:2-4:
"In my Father's house are many "mansions;" if it were not so, I would have told you. I go to prepare a place for you. And if I go to prepare a place for you, I will come again and receive you to Myself; that where I am you may be also. And where I go you know, and the way you know."

    As we connect this quote to our Dimensions, our world, and other worlds are a symbol of the Mansions Jesus says He is preparing. And He is always with us: we are aware of his presence, we are aware of the road we need to travel. Although many of us may already be saved, we have decided to come back to earth as incognitos to help mankind achieve salvation as a Whole. As it is written in Ecclesiastes 1:9-11:

"That which has been is what will be,
That which is done is what will be done,
And there is nothing new under the sun.
Is there anything of which it may be said,
"See, this is new"?

It has already been in ancient times before us.
There is no remembrance of former things
Nor will there be any remembrance of things
that are to come.
By those who will come after."

In these verses, we have the confirmation of the existence of reincarnation, and that all things have already happened but before we existed on this planet.

The Bible commentators Keil and Delitzsch wrote at the end of the 19th century a comment referring to the following sentence:

"It has already been in ancient times before us"

According to them, this sentence expresses,

".... A FORCE OF A HYPOTHETICAL ANTECEDENT..."

Therefore, we should not be surprised to read that our brain is a prototype: all knowledge is stored in it, and it is slowly disclosed on earth as we develop. An upcoming chapter titled The

Energy Cord will describe the storage in our brain.

Furthermore, an investigation performed by the Celestial Beings, concluded that all of us come from some form of energy that existed before the creation of the universes. They also concluded that all of us, even Allah, would not exist if that energy did not manifest in all there is, including human beings; this is our essence. As a result, we may be able to understand and accept, that we are prototypes: we are copies of previous beings, all designed by Superior and Powerful Celestial forces and that all information is stored in our brains, which is a concept already referred to as a *priori*.

Let us recall that the first Bible, (that is, scrolls) made many references to reincarnation. However, in the year 325 A.D., Emperor Constantine the Great, at the Council of Nicaea, decided to delete some passages he did not personally care for. He was followed by other emperors who removed still more. Fortunately, there is information that can help those of us who are interested to find out the truth about ourselves. In the

New Testament, there are symbols that cannot be removed. For example, the Resurrection of Jesus Christ is the greatest symbol of the fact that life goes on after death. The cause for our rejection of reincarnation has been described as having been inspired by the fact that we used to believe and are still believing, that it is more convenient or fair to correct our thoughts in just one lifetime. But just one lifetime, as we know, has never worked out. Moreover, many of us from all religions and secular backgrounds still do not believe in reincarnation. Among the "You only live once" crowd, we find not only harmless sensualists and average Joes, but murderers, thieves, rapists, and others who abuse human beings, and nature. Refusing to accept responsibility for their actions and thoughts, it must come as a shock to them at death when they realize that their thoughts and karma go with them.

    It is also about time we accept the fact that our thoughts reflect on all the universes and beyond.

Since energy is constantly reproducing copies of our past, we are definitely prototypes. All is stored in the Energy Cord.

## CHAPTER 24
# THE ENERGY CORD AND THE CODES

We know that the concept of reincarnation has been repressed in most cultures and is commonly disregarded altogether. However, reincarnation is a must for mankind to embrace, as a Whole.

Ultimately, it may not be necessary to believe in anything; just examining life and experiencing it may be enough. We have to consider that on earth everything is energy, all the way up to the Universe of Light. The reason is that the Dimension of the Universe of Light is beyond energy: it is Breath. Energy and breath work in cooperation with each other. The mission of breath is to connect our biological bodies to Spirit. We call that the Energy Cord. In the end there are two types of energy: material and cosmic. Material has to do with our universe, whereas cosmic has to do with the universe of Light.

Let's remember that we came from Light, which had to be transformed to what we call energy in order to suit our environment. Like breath, energy does not die or disappear into nothing. It is simply transformed in accordance with our needs, as we develop and go back to Breath; that is, we go back to Light. We have also read that special brain cells are a storage house where all our history is kept since our first arrival on earth up to our last lifetime.

How and why does this happen? It is written that energy is what maintains our survival on earth. Unfortunately, few of us realize that Spirit comes from the Universe of Light which as we know now, is Breath. Many of us prefer to cringe at the idea of Spirit. It seems easier to avoid the issue by saying that we don't believe. What we are actually saying is that we don't believe in energy, much less in breath. We must be aware that energy is everywhere, especially within us. Without energy, we would not exist. Some individuals will always run away from the truth.

Spiritual energy is what sustains our life.

During our journey on earth, we feed our brain cells based on all the lessons we are learning. The energy of our emotions, such as happiness and sorrow, contributes to our development. Spiritual energy is part of a Plan that gives us our power of living and is also known as the Energy Cord. It connects to the genes all the information we feed it with and transfers the information to special brain cells which are frozen in our genes, by a method unknown to us. Unlike other cells, which are renewed, the special brain cells are not renewed as they contain all the information of our past lives. Since Spirit is nonphysical, it mixes with crude matter, in this case, in the brain. The purpose is to record on diskettes our thoughts and impressions about all types of experiences that we go through in our lives. For that reason, we are all assigned a *code* and a *key* that no one can use but ourselves. This is the way that our Monitors (Superior Beings), beyond space and time, observe how we react and behave. They thereby discover our level of development and then proceed to help us with our needs for advancement.

In the brain is the encounter of our nonphysical with our mainly physical thoughts and emotions.

The Energy Cord has another task, which is to bring us back to beyond space and time when we die that is, when we astrally project. At the moment of death, it disconnects from the body and a beam of Light transports us to whichever dimension we are destined to go to, in accordance with our behavior on earth. But this event does not mean that Spirit leaves the body. The reality is that the Energy Cord was not in the body and, neither is spirit. This should be easy to understand when we think about how we plug in a TV set: The TV is not inside the electrical outlet.

There have been photographs taken of spirits leaving the bodies, while the deceased individuals appeared to be floating above a great fire on earth and, peacefully watching the event.
This helps us realize that there is no pain when we go through some forms of death; in a split second, we are transported by the Light to other dimensions at a speed that we are not aware of and the pain never materializes.

The task of the Cord is limited to time when we are in physical form, and lead us to see life after death as a continuation of our thoughts, independent of what dimension we are sent to. For that reason, I gave the example described in a previous chapter, of a communication received from my beloved friend after he passed away. In other words, once the Energy Cord disconnects from our physical bodies, we may be able to go anywhere, it depends on how advanced we are. We may be able to fly to any dimension in accordance with our thoughts and spiritual development and, above all with the help from the Light.

Secular people should ponder these truths when they receive such messages. Indeed, we are always in need of help even after we pass away, and of course, before. All of us are always in need of Love. And that form of communication can only be achieved with the help of True-Love.
It is interesting to note that Stephen Hawking, in a speech in 2017/18, informed mankind of its need to ride on a beam of light and go to other planets.

In the meantime, while we are on earth, the Energy Cords belongs only to us. If we choose to come back to earth it will be with us to start recording our development again.

Another function of the brain is to shut off the information stored in there, so that we will not be able to recall our past lives while we are in crude-matter form. Mankind is not prepared to recall such events, from one embodiment to the next, while we are on earth. We must understand how hard it would be to go through our past miseries and mistakes, such as torture, murder, betrayal, etc. To find out about our past lives, most of us have to wait until after we depart from our bodies. But there are exceptions. While on earth, the owner of the Cord, may be able to look at some of the information via the code implanted in him/her which contains the key to their development. This is done with permission from Beings beyond space and time and it depends on whether we, on earth, have achieved a certain level in our thought system.

We are warned not to believe everything we are told if we receive such information from other sources than our own. It is clear that genes and cells play a major role in our development and also in our reincarnation.

The role of the Energy Cord is to give us a picture of The Whole that has accumulated in the diskettes, which contains all the history of our many experiences on earth. This picture prepares all of us to become Authentic Humans. But to do this, all of us, whether religious or not, must love, respect and appreciate Allah's peaceful mission, as well as those of Jesus, Moses, Mohammed and all the other Powers known or unknown to us, since all of them have been working in cooperation with one another and without discrimination.

The reader may wonder when crude matter was planned and where it came into effect. It was planned before the Big Bang and came into effect in Atlanta.

## CHAPTER 25
## ATLANTA'S MISSIONS

Before proceeding to read, it may be necessary to imagine that we are watching a movie or reading a script. On the other hand, remember this is not science fiction. It is written that Light brought knowledge to the world. Therefore, a question arises: Does Light travel from its Source directly to us? We expect the answer to be "Yes," especially given that the Source is a Great Potential. However, we are not considering the interferences of "thoughts" that show up during this journey. What was unified is now split, and therefore guilt and all ego thoughts are about to have an encounter with the Source of their previous unification. The journey the Light takes seems to have reached its highest point in Atlanta, a Dimension where the consciousness totality was accomplished which led to the formation of atomic bonds. For that reason, some form of crude matter was first initiated before our existence. Atlanta Dimension is also where The First Constitution was initiated; where Solar Systems not yet quite known were established; where the human body, as we know it today, initiated its form as prototypes.

All was very well planned and happened before the Big Bang and Adam and Eve. The Beings in Atlanta were called Atlanteans. Some of them were called also Adams. All were androgynous. In other words, there was no physical contact in order to populate Atlanta with beings. We can imagine that reproduction was achieved in cooperation with their advanced thought system and the Divine. From there all is turned into reflections that bathe us with knowledge directly from the Creator of all Creations.

But let's not go so fast! There is more unexpected news. It is written that our world exists in an atomic area, together with many other worlds. Nevertheless, as described in a previous chapter all events happened first, as a rehearsal, in an artificial area. Then reflected in another universe, known as the 2$^{nd}$ Universe where Adam and Eve came into being, and later contributed to the development of our planet.

Let's relax and ponder: The reflections we receive in our planet are from the 2nd Universe, but before they were rehearsed in an artificial area. This is why it is mentioned that ours is a world of reflections. Since all events happened first in an artificial area then, the Life of Christ and everything in history are copies of those events.

This demonstrates again and again, what is written about A *Priori.* Often, we realize that the mission of the Celestial Beings, who were also intermediaries who participated in the writings of *The KB,* is similar to ours. Indeed, we are all on a mission, both here and there. All of us are doing research, scientific or not. They admit that they study particles and so do we. Theirs is, of course, a more advanced technology and their environment differs greatly from ours. As such, they have discovered a "Power" in their Dimension that is Unknown, even to them. It cannot be investigated, because everything created would disappear. Still, that power sends us signals that we are not able to decode.

This puzzles humanity very much. They wonder about our ignorance. We, on the other hand, wonder about the form and values of their existence.

We have read that in accordance with NASA research, there is already scientific evidence for alien life that is kept secret by the so-called elites who keep us in darkness for their own benefit. The information about their thought forms and their life styles would promote peace and a new understanding of who we are, where we are heading and above all, receptivity and respect for reincarnation.

At this time in human history perhaps, this should be a priority. But we have to be careful, other sources tell us that not all of them are peaceful. In spite of such warnings, we hope our alien friends would do us a great favor, if they somehow would show up on earth, in our TV sets, in Mars or somewhere else, in whatever form they have, not as incognitos. We may not be quite ready, but we are preparing ourselves not technologically but psychologically to go through a complete reversal in our thought system and lifestyle. They know our technology is not as advanced as theirs. Besides, most of them, if not all, are incombustible, therefore in some aspects they cannot be hurt.

We already know they have no intention of harming or invading us. The stress, the dismay, the loneliness, and confusion that mankind is going through, also caused by cosmic anxiety, at a time of relative peace, is astounding.
Such a state in the human condition was implemented by the System for the benefit of mankind. It gives us chances to choose peace or war within ourselves. Again, let's recall that it is not God that causes our problems. We are the ones who created the split of our unified consciousness and now we have to unify.

Ask yourself: Do I still hold grudges against someone I met years or decades ago or even right now? You can clear such feelings yourself, especially if you realize the damage you are causing while on earth, and will continue after death. You can repeat to yourself, as often as necessary that "Love is always the answer". Or ask to remember Love. You can also imagine that person or persons standing in front of you, and light floating from your heart to the other individual's heart.

The System, like the intensive stress and confusion, mentioned above, started to be effective on earth after the year 2000. At the beginning of the 20$^{th}$ century, the cosmic waves sent to us were too strong for some of us to handle, particularly non-believers and those who had not sufficiently developed. Therefore, causing cosmic anxiety. Do not despair. All of us are being guided towards a better future. There are flowers in the garden. For that reason, we are reminded that when the system was first designed in the Atlanta dimension, by Beings that existed before our planet, laws, rules and regulations, such as, Love and respect, were then initiated. The system has nothing to do with what the elites on this planet have implemented, in order to contradict what was designed before our existence. Although we may have difficulty following some rules and regulations, let's not forget that our present human condition was initiated by all of us when our consciousness split. Now, we are being offered a peaceful way to recover which starts with the individual, then with the masses and that is why it takes time. It is up to us to accept it or not.

Reflect on this: What have we done since then?

We know that all events are prepared in accordance with the development of the masses, and for the benefit of mankind. Surely, in the distant past, we went through wars, slavery, starvation and other miseries. Although some of these conditions still exist in many parts of the world, at present we also have abundance like never before. At the same time, we continue to promote wars especially within ourselves.

Amidst this confusion, we have to wonder: What does Atlanta still have to do with our formation, and above all with our future?

May be the reader will be surprised to find out about Allah's mission in Atlanta.

## CHAPTER 26
### ATLANTA DIMENSION AND ALLAH

In principle, no one knows where Atlanta was located and how it came into being. However, we must remember that there were Powerful Beings before our existence. But now we learn, for the first time in history that Allah's Dimension was activated in Atlanta before the existence of our planet. Later on, Adam and Eve received engraftment from Atlanta's genes; they represent the "Power of God" and are called "God's genes." This does not mean that God has genes like humans do; it means that mankind has inherited His Power. In the future, all of us will increasingly carry those genes and, having received such Power, we'll be considered as gods. But we are not God. Allah's Mission is to prepare us for these events, so that we will discover the great potential within us to be able to create even universes, by unifying our consciousness.

There is, however, another aspect of the information about God's genes. We have read that Allah is the God of His creations, meaning crude matter.

Later we learned that Adam and Eve were engrafted not with Allah's genes but with God's. This means that the Celestial Beings are aware of a Creator of All Creations, who gave some of His Power to Allah.

It is also written that God's Genes appear to have been lost, but now they have been found. This is explained in the next chapter. If we have misgivings about the story of Atlanta, it may help to consider that there were Powerful Beings before our existence and, even more advanced civilizations, the remnants of which still exist.

They are expected to have built, among other structures, the nuclear reactor in Gabon, Africa, mentioned in earlier chapter. At present, some individuals claim that Mother Nature built the reactor, and even call it a phenomenon—this is another way to convince us not to ponder and not let the truth come out. We are aware that Atlanteans were known for using their thought-powers in a way that could move mountains.

All of us have the potential to use our thought-powers in the same way but, for now, we've yet to reach that stage. Our confusion, fear and guilt hold us back, until we have the necessary willpower to defeat it.

Whatever happened to that dimension called Atlanta, which of course had to be beyond the earth? It is described as the center--- that is, the focal point--- that led to crude matter. Although the researchers in *The KB* could not perform detailed analysis, because the area is not opened, they accept that all the information, all the energies, all the knowledge are unified in there as Light, and give rise to what they understand as consciousness.

How does the information get in there? We know that information comes from a Thought that is the Source of all there is: LIGHT. Certainly, thoughts have to travel from that Source. Afterwards, they are filtered to that space which is where duality (meaning ego thoughts) and non-duality (True-Love) was first processed. There is a reference to this concept as described by scientist David Bohm, a few pages ahead.

There is a Creator, who created crude matter and has chosen a secret and secluded space that we may call Atlanta, in order to disseminate knowledge and initiate plans for our formation. As we know, this Creator is Allah. All that is created in that secret area is manifested from the Universe of Light. It is the Universe of Light that emits reflections to all of us.

Reflections enabled Allah to structure, organize and, later bring into effect Laws, Rules and Regulations after the existence of our planet.

It was in Atlanta that Allah participated in the structure of the First Constitution with Laws of the Universe, all leading to crude matter in the form of planets and us. In these Laws, there are Commandments similar to those of Moses' and Holy Books from all traditions. This include respect and love for the humans, animals, Mother Nature----and yes, even enemies. Respect and responsibility are emphasized throughout *The Text* embraced by mankind without the use of force. Sometimes, the reader feels like he/she is reading the Christian Bible, but with different words and energy. The more we read, the more we find confirmation of our past lives and above all, that we are prototype. Indeed, we learn that our physical body is a prototype of Atlanta, and that Atlanteans were androgynous. The authors anticipate reaction to these concepts. They are aware that they may be seen as myths. Although humanity has long mentioned stories about its origin and gods, the problem with myth is that there is no distinction between what is true and what is false.

Still, now in the 21$^{st}$ century with our advances in education and technology, we are able to discern truth, and the thought system, if we have open minds. We have to accept that there have been and continue to be civilizations far more advanced than ours and that we all come from the very same Source; this is our Ultimate Reality. We know that reflections bring information and therefore communication from the Divine and they exist because crude matter is not real. The Reality that emits reflections, abides beyond what we can see. All of us are reflections of the unseen, just as Atlanteans used to be. But they used the Reflections they received to become powerful.

For all its power, the Atlantean civilization did not last.

Let's recall that in principle, Atlanta dimension was never located on our Planet. However, some of the priests formed an underwater civilization after the formation of the earth. Those beings are called Atlantis.

We have read that the 1st Constitution originated in Atlanta before our planet and universes began. The question is: How? It is written that their system of thought was programmed to receive the power of Natural Energies. This means they allowed the Divine to orient their thoughts. Allah hopes that we will, one day, be able to do the same! This is his last hope.

Atlanteans were so successful that they created the first known Golden Age, which lasted for an indefinite period of time until it started to degenerate.

CHAPTER 27

## WHY DID ATLANTA DEGENERATE?

What happened then? As it is written, the priests were the ones who maintained the Atlanta civilization. They used the Natural Powers which come from the Divine, to attract energies through their brains which must have reflected to other Beings. In spite of having the same genes, the virtues of some beings who had come from other regions started to degenerate, until they lost contact with the Divine and therefore lost their power. In other words, androgynous beings that joined them from other cultures must have had problems adjusting to the new environment.

Does this sound familiar, especially if we consider that history repeats itself? Not even their advanced technology could save them. They refused to follow the Divine just as Lucifer and all of us had done. In other words, we can imagine that even androgynous beings, rebelled. Consequently, their genes which had God's power dissipated. Herein lies, again, the Power of the

Creator of All Creations that some of us call God.

As previously mentioned, God's genes were then lost. Let's put it this way: under the circumstances they had to be lost: They lost their contact with the Divine. Now it seems to be our mission to search for those lost genes. But, we must have achieved great success, because the lost genes have been found. And now Allah has assembled them in an area, beyond planets and universes and is waiting for us to join him there and receive God's Power again. In the meantime, we have to consider that the First Constitution led to their degeneration.

Why? Just two of the rules imposed on them described the responsibility of mothers and fathers to take care of all the children in their community. Besides, they had to share in the same manner and without any discrimination, all there was. Other rules have to do with family values and, with the fact that if they did not follow the rules they would have to reincarnate. These rules completely shook up their thought system and makes us think that since their consciousness was unified then, it started to split --- giving us the idea that the thought of separation started in the Atlanta dimension.

But how? First of all, a unified consciousness does not need ladders and dimensions to develop since they are connected to the Divine as One. Furthermore, a unified consciousness does not need to be reminded of Love, because the Divine is Love. Once that connection with the Divine disappeared, they started to think in terms of dimensions, that is, different levels of experiencing separation. This was accomplished through reflections coming from many ladders and going through different dimensions, such as, the biological dimension (meaning physical contact) and immortality dimension just as we do today, on earth. And this event completely turned their thought system upside down. Let's repeat that they started to use evolution ladders for the first time in order to adjust their thoughts according to their needs, instead of using the power of the Divine: That destroyed their capacity to move mountains, among other wonders. Other Constitutions followed, which led to still more individual and family rules. They all failed.

In spite of the fact that Love was already mentioned in their Constitution, it was necessary to bring Jesus to our planet to introduce mankind to the concept and the experience of Love. According to what is written, many civilizations were destroyed, due to the way rules were interpreted and the revolution setup into their thought system in a situation where they had no choice: this eventually led to their total destruction.

Reflect on these sentences: They did not have the necessary willpower to handle their thoughts without the presence of the Divine.

This was a scenario to prepare crude matter in the future for the Big Bang, Adam and Eve and biological beings, like us.

In addition, it was also a scenario to put into effect free will, so that, future beings like us, could choose. What we do with our freedom is up to us. As we know, so far it has not worked either. Now, Allah is asking for our cooperation, so that we assist in his 4th Plan, which means, a new world. We are also informed that there are 600 Atlantean Priests presently living, as incognitos, on the earth and helping us achieve our mission.

The question is: Why is Allah trying to get us back to the ways of the Golden Civilization Dimension of Atlanta, when he knows it failed? He has tried three times to bring us together with his Plans, namely:

1st: Masters of the Ancient Far East.
2nd: Moses
3rd: Jesus and Mohammed

They all failed to completely unify our consciousness, in spite of the fact that free will has been in effect. Humans were not quite ready to refine and expand their feelings, especially those inspired by ego.

At present, Allah is using Light-Photon-Cyclone Technique, for the first and last time, in order to implement what he calls his Fourth and final Plan, which started in the year 2000, as we know. And this is his last hope to succeed creating perfect human beings since we are running out of time. He expects that the love and tolerance that we see in the

West, together with his new Technique, will help humanity avoid Atlantean-like destruction.

The slogans like love, patience, unity, have been repeated in every life-cycle. They are necessary so that our 64 Billion cells unify with our brains and become very powerful cell brains. Then we can progress to the infinite. By the $30^{th}$ century if all goes well, after climbing up many ladders, all, or almost all inhabitants of this planet will become civilized, and proceed to other galaxies in a likely manner. Our consciousness will be unified to the point that we will live in relative peace and will be able to govern ourselves without wars in the world or within ourselves. Then, we'll become perfect Human Beings, even for a short time before we go on to other wonderful worlds that we will create with our advanced thought system. Hopefully, all galaxies will benefit from our development: as we know thoughts have no frontiers.

Do not be discouraged because the foundations for The Golden Age are being set up and successfully achieved right now until the end of the 22nd century.

It is written that these concepts have yet to be accepted, much less anticipated by most of us, particularly by a great majority in the Muslim community.
In the end, we know that it will be just a question of time.

## CHAPTER 28
## TIME IS AN ILLUSION

We must take into consideration what we know about the concept of time: all there is, is an instant.

Time is an illusion that we invented to keep us focused on the terrestrial. One instant in some galaxies is equivalent to 30 years in our world.

This is a reminder of the film *Time Machine*, inspired by H.G. Wells' science fiction novel, which was a success during the 20th century. A machine was invented which allowed us to travel to the past or to the future in time. All is written and recorded. The task of the Time Machine is to keep moving along as the scenes unfold like in a movie. It is a symbol that time does not move but we do! As described in another chapter, the concept of twin universes, fits right in here: One universe, known as positive, moves forward: this means that we are always advancing. The other, (negative) moves backward. But, sooner or later, we are going Home—back to where we came from. Back to the One Atom. This will happen because the negative universe is a mirage of the positive.

What this means is that humans distorted the truth. The positive universe is real. It cannot be changed: God just IS.

This is also a reminder of what is written about the fact that all our thoughts from our past lives and life-cycles are stored in archives beyond space and time. They can provide us with an understanding of cause and effect. All religious books come from the same source; That is, the concepts and ideas are tied in. Besides, let's recall that all things are one inside the other, including universes. This means that all is unified and cannot be separated. It is up to us to choose which road to follow. We have enough information to realize the importance of thoughts and that they create universes. Each universe is somehow connected to a different center, which then is attached to a Single Center. It is from here that they receive directions. It is further explained that the explosions we call the Big Bang are caused by natural movements that happened before times. But before that event, there were Three Universes one inside the other that completed a Whole. These details lead us to understand the importance of thoughts and that One Thought attracts the others in this case, to form a countless number of universes. These events happened before Fire, Light and Sound were created.

In the meantime, after much research, performed by the Celestial Beings, it was understood that they came from a Technological Dimension which brought all into existence. Sometime in the future, which may be sooner than we expected, mankind will have to go through profound meditations and realize, for ever and ever, that nothing is separate. It is also written that the information about our formation is described in all the Bibles but the interpretation is very difficult. Consequently, it was known far in advance that all cycles were going to fail. All is programmed little by little as we progress and our thoughts are being watched.

David Bohm, the well-known theoretical physicist, wrote in *Wholeness and The Implicate Order*, that thoughts are filtered through what he called "*The* Implicate Order." Then are carried through the holomovement which is where our duality (ego) is processed, and non-duality, that is unity and Wholeness, is remembered. Therefore, we may conclude that it is here where our guides, such as Jesus, Moses, Mohammed, and others, help us.

Our thoughts (good, bad and ugly) expand into the infinite. In this process, they are always being "filtered" so that purification takes place. This happens while we are alive and also at death. Filtration leads to purification which is unification.

The Unknown Power is a unification of this process, which was essential for the formation of crude matter. Regardless of what planet we are on, our thoughts always play a major role in every event. It is written that there are all sorts of planets, some with cats, others with dogs etc., and that all relationships are connected to the Divine. Furthermore, they advise us to stop reproducing, for which no reason is given and to be patient. We are also reminded that our pets are on earth to learn to inhabit, one day, a human form and to come and join us wherever we may be. At the same time, we are on earth to learn to become authentic humans; that is, as we know, when our brain unifies with our heart, which may seem to take centuries but, in the end, may take only an instant. It all depends on how we handle the soup we have created.

CHAPTER 29

## UNIVERSES ARE ONE INSIDE THE OTHER. CAN WE ELIMINATE EVIL?

The fundamental thought to understand the unification of all things is that there is no separation. Even universes are one inside the other. This concept of no separation facilitates our understanding of unification. In other words, we learn that they occupy the same space. Just like soup! What kind of communication exists among them? As an author inspired by what is beyond the physical, often my energy goes up and down. My temperature changes. By the time I see my doctor, I find out that I am perfectly all right. The doctor insists that it is natural for energy and temperature to oscillate. What does really happen? Since there is no separation in any event we experience, they are therefore connected for some reason unknown to us. While I am trying to have order and discipline in order to write, there is a law of attraction caused by gravitation leading to what is known in new physics, as entropy.

The propose of entropy is to cause chaos and disorder in our thought system. This activity is what I have previously described as a push, and provocation. In other words, chaos and disorder can sometimes help us organize ourselves, and improve our life styles, if we are able to calm down. This means that entropy is positive and negative. The concepts just described are known by physicists as thermodynamics that have forced the formation of twin universes. All caused by the soup we have created. One of the universes is orderly and of course, positive: It is our universe. The other is negative; It is where disorder predominates—It is a copy of the positive but, it looks like a ghost. If we think we can eliminate one, we have to eliminate the other for, they are entangled. Here, we have the confirmation that there is no separation. Likewise, if we want to eliminate evil, we have to eliminate the good, and vice versa. Unaware of the implications of this concept until recently, mankind's major dilemma is how can we solve this seemingly difficult situation? The answer is given in religious and no religious writings, including *in The KB.*

Consider this: Since there is no separation, and one thing is inside the other, there seems to be some unity between them in a way that one influences the other, for better or for worse. We need to see both sides of the coin so to speak, and try and balance our lives. What keeps that soup active is our thoughts. We have to consider that all events are scheduled to happen at a specific time to activate our brains so that we take some action hopefully for the benefit of humanity. Good and evil, darkness and light, and what is known in Chinese philosophy as yin and yang exist in our world and are interconnected. To achieve success, we have to be able to handle both and find some balance. We need to relax. In other words, we need a push which can be in the form of a prayer, a nap, a walk by the ocean, remembrance of love, and forgiveness or even a visit to the doctor. In short, whatever we choose to do, make sure that we do not suffer from exhaustion of any kind. The Cosmos is always in communication with us, and we too are in communication with all galaxies, all planets. It is when we relax that the information is more active and we may be able to avoid chaos, as well as lack of balance. In other words, we can calm down evil by simply taking good care of our physical and spiritual condition.

We need proper foods and proper exercise, without exaggeration, so that our attitude adapts to our needs. We hear about these recommendations over and over again, from doctors, family members, friends, and even the media. We have read that all humans are on a mission. One of the physicists' mission was to have discovered that all good and bad thoughts have been and will continue to be universally conserved. Conservation is accomplished by the Energy Cord. The system which was implemented before Adam and Eve, will go on until we choose to unify our consciousness, and Conservation is a reminder that thoughts do not evaporate unto nothingness. From the point of view of spirituality, we may consider that what leads to obstruction and disorder is ego interference, call it evil or whatever. We are back to the same conclusion: we cannot eradicate the ego, but we must learn to peacefully handle our emotions, so that its influence decreases. Then, we can exist in a more harmonious state in our positive universe and beyond. The concept that energy/thoughts are universally conserved, contributes to our understanding that life goes on here, there and everywhere in different forms, repeating itself in on-going cycles.

In 1843, the English author, Charles Dickens, published his book titled Christmas Carol: a ghost story of Christmas which became a famous movie in the 20th century. It is the story of stingy man whose past showed up in the movie as a ghost and changed him in the end to be kind and gentle.
Jorge Amado, a Brazilian author, wrote "Dona Flor and Her Two Husbands" which turned out to be also a famous movie. In this case, her first husband was no good. He died and after she remarried, she started to miss him. He, on the hand, decided to show up on earth as a ghost and naked, to call her attention to the good times they had together. Millions of people are afraid of

ghosts. However, millions of people saw the above mentioned movies and loved them. They must have been very relaxed and had a good night's sleep just before they saw the movies.
Their attitude must have been of a dreamer, who is having problems accepting the realities of life.

We have read that earth is a laboratory. We choose to come here to learn about the unity of all there is and the need to unify. We are also learning that positive and negative universes occupy the same space; All is entangled. This idea helps us realize that in order to accomplish our mission in accordance with thermodynamics laws, we have to work with both positive (Love/God) and negative elements (ego). We have to keep on working towards peaceful solutions of all aspects of our lives so that we'll purify the earth and ourselves, and may be, avoid coming back. The conclusion is that new physics also lead us to the concept of reincarnation, and that energy/thoughts are conserved for that reason. It is thanks to the conservation of our thoughts that we can compare our past lives and program our return to earth if we want. We may then conclude that if we have a quarrel with someone, a divorce, a misunderstanding, we must not believe that by saying "Good-Bye," we will let go of that person. Remember that all thoughts occupy the same space and a dance is going on. We may need to go face to face with that individual or not, but we have to handle the situation remembering Love and, sometimes forgiveness is necessary. Whatever we imagine we do to others, we are doing to ourselves. We are mirrors to each other, since we occupy the same space. Life is on-going on earth and beyond. This is science, this is spirituality. We will meet again and again until we achieve a unified consciousness.

So, is the dance of life, as exemplified by god Shiva. Although his name literarily means the kind and friendly one, he has 3 faces and combines in himself contradictory qualities of both destroyer and restorer. What does Shiva destroy? Ignorance. This is considered a great blessing in Hindu culture. Indeed, what better accomplishment could there be during our short visit on earth, than to learn to destroy the erroneous concept we've of ourselves?

How can we destroy such ignorance, in other words, how can we work towards our salvation? The Hindu culture teaches the use of Yoga and meditation, other cultures teach payers, more primitive cultures teach sacrifice. Whichever path we choose, we must always act and react. We cannot and must not isolate ourselves completely, and even if we try, our thoughts will always be in charge of our lives, and we have to learn to handle them. We have to attract the negativity close enough to allow the light to illuminate our minds and wipe out our ignorance about the Truth.

Our mission is planned and designed so that we succeed in the illumination of the path we are threading. Who is the designer?

## CHAPTER 30
### WHO DESIGNED OUR SALVATION PLAN?

Our plan for salvation was designed by the Unknown with the participation of Allah and us. Remember that there is no separation. We know that our thought of separation from the Unified Consciousness which started before the Big Bang, caused so much guilt and self-punishment that our consciousness was fragmented. It is our mission to recover and realize Mass Consciousness so that we can return to our former Unity. In the meantime, according to what is written, we actually choose the circumstances of our lives on earth. How and why can we do that? First of all, we do this before we come to earth in order to learn the value of our return Home. We must also consider our needs, based on previous embodiments, which can be done only when we are not in physical form. Herein lies the advantages of looking at our past lives before we come to earth again. No one interferes with our choices. Somehow, free will has always been of our essence. We have read that fragmentation causes duality in our thoughts, such as: good, bad, handsome, ugly and so forth. Duality always represents choices.

But the truth is that although some of us do not need to choose, because we have already chosen to be united as per the Love of Jesus, others have yet to see the Light. All we need to do is to remember the Truth. And sometimes, the truth can hurt.

It is written that we were the first to reach God, whereas the Celestial Beings who participate in the writings of *The KB* have yet to be that successful. This is one of the reasons why Jesus Christ came to earth-- to help us remember! So far, most of us have chosen to forget. In our deep sleep, we forget that we have already been forgiven. Certainly, a Loving God would not set up such a cruel plan especially with the intention of making it last forever. We have to stop blaming others for our problems.

For this reason, an important question arises: Why did the Creator of All Creations allow us to design the plan of salvation in cooperation with Allah? The answer is that *free will and the ego* were created as a consequence of the events in Atlanta when our consciousness seems to have split and no God interferes with the problems we have created, in this case: separation. The Truth is that no one can separate from something that exists within them. So, we are free to hate, kill and so forth. But we can also love to an infinite extent, and realize the Power we've within us. We can use our thoughts constructively, as we very well know. We are the ones who have to undo what we invented. The success of free will depends upon the recognition of our unity with the Divine. This means that when we realize that our will and God's are the same (whatever concept we have of Him), we unite and Total Will is realized. Then, we may conclude there is no further need to choose.

On the other hand, The Divine continues to use all of us to convey His messages. In short, we are all His messengers, whether we believe it or not and, also His children. In the case of *The KB*, The Unknown spoke also through Allah, and many other Powers, as He has done before. These are the channels that have been chosen to tell us the truth. Do not be confused. Allah is confident and sincere in making it clear that although he is considered by his followers to be the God of the dimension he created, such as crude matter, there is a Power that provided him with the energy to create. He calls this Power "The Unknown."

And it is this Power that may be considered The Creator of All Creations. This does not affect the love Allah has for mankind, as well as the love that many people have for him. But we must understand that his mission is temporary and see him as a peaceful and truthful messenger. After all is said and done, as we know, there is only One God: That is to say, there is but One Center, One Photon, One Nucleus, One Atom. Now we understand why words are but symbols.

Following His guidance, humanity is always creating. We may become so powerful that we, too, will become as worship-worthy as Gods. His guidance always lifts us up.

The truth is that we humans have long searched for spiritual unity since our beginnings. We have worshipped tribal Gods and divine kings, not to mention animal-headed gods. There were also phallic and fertility cults. For those who loved nature, there were gods and goddesses of the moon, ocean, the earth. However, in the 20th century, a new form of worship was born. It had nothing to do with spiritual unity or the Divine; it became known as state worship, under Communism and Hitler, with the aim of eliminating religions and dominating the entire world. The good news is that this type of "worship" will endure only until mankind accepts *The KB* as its guide. Then, all beings will learn to rule themselves.

There will still be some form of a State, but not the kind we are used to. For now, we are asked not to worship any religion or any State, but rather to keep some examples of their actions and deeds in mind and, to meditate on them. One of the aims of what is written is to explain the dynamics that the Hierarchy beyond the terrestrial plays, which have a major role in the development of our thoughts. In the future, humans will advance in such a way that we'll create universes, become Superior Beings and, as just noted, may even be considered gods by the onlookers from other planets or, even from our planet. Furthermore, since our salvation has already been accomplished, at least by some of us, it behooves humanity to accept this truth and learn from it. This is our choice and our problem, which we have the responsibility to solve. In the meantime, since we are living in the illusion of time, the whole process of salvation seems to be taking centuries, during which Mevlana always played a major role and continues to help us.

We already know that only in the 30th century, will we reach the Golden Age. But that will not be our complete salvation: it will be followed by the Age of Light. We came from Light, we'll go back to Light.

CHAPTER 31
## WHO IS MEVLANA?

Mevlana is a beautiful woman who received the information described in *The KB* in the 20th century with the help of The Technique, already mentioned. As we know, this technique consists of a Photon travelling at a speed unknown on earth. It is a power that opposes matter and is beyond energy: It is breath. Therefore, it can only be from The Creator of all Creations. It cannot be measured the way we measure the speed of light. It even has an effect on the way we receive energies as we go on reading *The Text*.

How was *The KB* communicated to Mevlana? By Archangel Gabriel, who identifies himself as Mustafa Molla. But the information was also sent by very powerful intermediaries from many dimensions and even beyond. She was always very aware of what she was writing, and also wrote several chapters in *The Text* under the name of Pen of Golden Age, as well as books about *The KB*.

Mevlana clarifies that she is not a medium but a missionary, and that all of us are on a mission. Her full name is Vedia Bulent Onsu Corak. She was born in 1923 in Turkey, the land of Ataturk, the founder of modern Turkey and the 1st President (1881-1938.) His inspiration continues to have an effect on its people. His slogan was: Peace at home, peace in the world. It is thanks to him that women in Turkey are allowed to vote.

Mevlana has great energy and is a True-Loving individual. Humanity may not be aware that the Love coming from her cells is necessary for us to advance. Her aura was reduced drastically, so that she could come to earth. She is Divine Light, and claims to be a reincarnation of the well-known 13th century Persian Sufi mystic, Rumi. Her sincerity is blazingly apparent. When she started to get the information to write *The Text* in the form of messages, she had doubts about their origin and decided to tear them up. But the Celestial Beings insisted, reminding her that there was a Covenant. This was the beginning of the dictation of *The Knowledge Book*. We are grateful to her, for she has chosen to come to earth to make us reflect on the continuity of life, the importance of our thoughts and, certainly reincarnation.

Mevlana is a unique individual and is also one of the Sixes, a group of very advanced Beings who were first engrafted with God's genes. We know some of them: Moses, Jesus, Mohammed. They are all on earth as veiled individuals. Although they know who they are, they keep it a secret among themselves. Only Mevlana is known. She has chosen to come out of the closet that she has existed on earth for decades, not only by writing the dictation of *The KB* by hand which took her 12 years, but also by letting us know about her past.

# CHAPTER 32
## WHY ARE HUMANS COMING OUT OF THEIR CLOSET?

It is our need to accelerate our evolution that propels us to come out of the closet. This is the reason why Mevlana became the scriber of *The Text*. However, we are now facing a very bumpy road: what was hidden before, has now been made visible, consequently we become more discriminative. We know that all events happening in the world are scheduled in accordance with a Plan set up by Celestial Beings. Here, again, is the proof that history repeats itself; instead of uniting we continue to segregate ourselves. Criticism of Mevlana's openness is eminent in some cycles, even within the Muslim community. We point fingers at others, instead of looking inward. This is the chaos we choose to impose on ourselves, over and over again as we go through many life-cycles and refuse to accept the truths. As our consciousness opens up, some humans are taking advantage of our exposure with revenge.

For too long we have been telling lies to ourselves and to the world about our true feelings. Now we feel so relieved about our previous condition that we may get a glimpse of the cause and too often concentrate with revenge on the effect. This may lead to turmoil in our consciousness and even to violence. Let's remember that we are always being guided and helped, so that we can reverse our thoughts.

Philosophers, psychologists, psychiatrist, along with other professionals and lay people are struggling to define consciousness. In the meantime, we've read in the chapter titled Descartes that to be conscious is to think. And in the chapter titled The Big Bang it is written that Light illuminates our thoughts and supplies knowledge to our consciousness. It is up to us to use the power of our creative thoughts to unify.

When the 1st Cosmic Age started in the 20th Century, we were wondering what was going to happen to the nuclear family, which consisted of mother, father and children. We also wondered about physical abuse in the families, churches and everywhere. However, all was kept secret. Now in the 21$^{st}$ century, whether we accept it or not, we find out that we are all involved in the 2$^{nd}$ Cosmic Age of our evolution towards the Age of Light. For that reason, changes have to happen to our thought system and in society. For that reason, we are receiving strong cosmic currents, and even "Energy Pores" which help us grasp the necessary knowledge to advance.

    We have the choice to let fear make our life miserable or, to let our hearts lead us to better worlds. Everyone is influenced by these currents. For example, many families now are constituted by two daddies and children or, two mommies and children. The fact that we've surrogates, test-tube babies and gay parents is redefining what a family is and also causing us to ponder. New words, new expressions, new meanings, new technology as well as physical abuse of children, men and women, that may have happened even decades ago, are now coming to light. There is so much information and knowledge reflecting on us by the Light that people's consciousness is shattered. Now, we have a chance to really examine our consciousness. It is hard to face the truths. Dangerous drugs and mental health problems are forcing the opening of mental institutions. We are our own worst enemies, we all know this. We do not take care of ourselves. We do not choose to focus within, we prefer to keep up with the Joneses! While all of these events are going on, respect and responsibility have declined drastically. Words like God and Love have almost disappeared from our vocabulary and may even be forbidden in some environments.

In the West, this is happening in an atmosphere of relative peace while in many other parts of the world, slavery continues to be part of people's lives. Yet, too many people applaud such a life-style. In some cultures, to this day, men and women are assassinated or, dismissed from society if they marry for love. Wars are always going on in the hope that people can improve their lives and start anew. Based on what we have read, the Plan has been set up to help us get out of the prisons that we have built in and around ourselves: It has been set up to allow us to choose peace or war.

Remember chapter 5, about the Devil?

We have read that to be conscious is to think and that Light supplies knowledge to our consciousness. When the unity of knowledge is achieved, all of us will be unified as a Whole. This can be achieved right now if we let ourselves come out of the dark closet we placed ourselves in and, instead, allow the Light to shine. Then, we conclude there is no separation; Light shines on all there is. In the end, all of us want to advance. However, as we take a step forward, we may take many steps backwards. For instance, parents must examine their consciousness. Too often they choose to lie to their children, without realizing that children need an environment of consistency. Otherwise they will be confused about what is true and what is false and may rebel, sooner or later. We have the example of what happened during the attack on 9/11 at the World Trade center, in New York City. Many parents and teachers decided to tell the children that "It was an accident."

Too many of us do not like the truth. Some readers will not like what is written even in this book: it reminds all of us the need to discipline ourselves, to take responsibility, to respect others, and to remember Love.

This is The Fourth and last Plan of Allah which started in the year 2000, as we know and will go on producing chaos, as long as we wish.

All of us must listen to the Great Power within us! But to do that we must awaken, and Love is necessary.

## CHAPTER 33
## **THE SLEEPING GIANT**

In the Bible, God has many names. In *The KB*, Allah is sometimes identified as Matu, other times as The Lord, or Serdar, other times also as (O), the Initial Creator (referring to crude matter). But (O) is also identified as the Supreme Creator, adding that, one day, all of us will be like Him.

As we have read, in the final analysis there are Three Creators, as there have been other Gods throughout history. But the Powers that created crude matter have nothing to do with technology, because technology comes from the Divine.

Based on this information, we are able to conclude that The Creator of all Creations has always been in charge of all there is, before and after the Big Bang.

It is also written that Superior Beings work hard to prevent our insanity from destroying our planet. And there is no possibility that we will be invaded by beings from beyond space and time. Still, some entities from areas beyond galaxies where love is nonexistent, need to be embodied and come to earth to learn about our values. They may have difficulty adjusting to our thought forms and that may be the cause of violence on our planet. This is one of the reasons why we need to achieve a unified consciousness in order to improve our thoughts and reflect them to other galaxies and even beyond.

We must appreciate the power of our values and existence.

For that reason, we must understand that mankind is advancing to realms beyond galaxies that are beyond crude matter, beyond ego. Love was created so that consciousness unifies as Whole because all of us share a "Particle" from the Divine, and that means the consciousness of all beings from all galaxies will be unified, sooner or later.

In the Bible, there are several references to events that happened before the world began.

For example, Peter 1:20, referring to Jesus Christ, mentions: "He indeed was foreordained before the foundation of the world, but was manifested in these last times for you…"

Quotes like this open our eyes to the fact that only a Great Unified Mind could have created an ongoing vortex of thoughts; That is, a Dance of Life! Without a Thinker to think a thought, there would be no Thought. Therefore, there would be no planets, galaxies--- in short, no living things.

Our thoughts are what cause Creation.

Since the beginning of our existence, we've allowed ourselves to be manipulated by fear, hate, guilt, anger and above all, by false love. Therefore, we must direct our thoughts in a different way, by reversing them, so that humanity may develop and advance as quickly as possible. We can make ego our worst enemy, or we can learn from it, and turning our lives around for the betterment of all.

We know that Allah is the Lord of our medium, meaning our world of crude matter. His mission is limited to space and time. Once he accomplishes his temporary mission with us, he leaves us to handle the cosmos ourselves while he goes to other dimensions. Hereafter, we will be able to realize our Infinite

Potential, thanks to the development of our thought system, and rule ourselves. We will proceed in a unified manner to many galaxies, and even beyond galaxies. We too will be called gods, as we will form new universes with our advanced thought system, as previously mentioned.

Let's meditate, again, on the following quote:

> "The religion of the future will
> be cosmic religion.
> It will transcend a personal God and
> Avoid dogma and theology."
>
> Albert Einstein

We will emerge from the medium we placed ourselves in, which is the box of our dream of separation. This is an important type of conditioning that we have to learn to handle. Then, we'll go to our greater destination, beyond the system that we invented--- that is, beyond pain, time, form, galaxies, dimensions; beyond cause and effect, beyond reincarnations. In short, it is a state beyond concepts and words, in which we realize that God, The Unknown, is not outside of ourselves but within. When we take this monumental step, it will mark the transition from the terrestrial to universal and beyond. But this will not begin to happen until we reach the 7$^{th}$ dimension, and the Beyond.

Let's remember what Jesus said in John 15:5: "I am the vine, you are the branches. He who abides in Me and I in him, bears much fruit; for without me you can do nothing."

And in John 14:12: "Most assuredly, I say to you, he who believes in Me, the works that I do he will do also; and greater works than these will he do, because I go to my Father."

It is also interesting to note that *The KB* mentions we, who were created by Allah as crude matter, will one day create much more advanced and better beings than he did. Indeed, it is staggering to realize that we are sleeping giants. When we wake up, we will create universes and much more.

For a while, the West will play a major role in our progress as explained in the next chapter.

## CHAPTER 34

## THE MISSION OF THE WEST

We are asked to accelerate the promotion of ideas of *The KB* to all the corners of the world, especially to the West. Why the West? Because the Celestial Beings are aware that not everyone is ready to accept the concepts described in *The Text.* They must have concluded that the West is more evolved and prepared to divulge it. The truth is that we have set the stage for Love, tolerance, humanness. These, as we know, are the slogans necessary for unification, leading to logic and reason. They have been repeated in every life-cycle on our planet always hoping to contribute to our evolution. Now with the help of Light-Photon-Cyclone Technique, the Celestial Beings hope humanity will open their eyes to the great potential within themselves to love and to create even new universes populated with Beings of unknown physical characteristics, capable of a harmonious existence. This is a great victory of our very often difficult process of maintaining freedom, achieved at the cost of a lot of pain.

It is previously mentioned that those of us who read just the 1st Fascicule will automatically be connected to the aura of *The Text*. But not everybody has access to it. Therefore, a special strategy has been set up. It consists of many members, from reflections centers with very powerful brains. They are placed in groups in technological and social areas in all continents of our planet, and also Turkey.

What is their mission? To reflect programs to save the planet, and expand the reflection among us humans. The aim is to help those who have not read even the 1st fascicule to be connected to the aura. Like this, they will hopefully awaken and contribute to its promotion together with those who, in the future will read *The Text*. Of course, those people receiving the messages from the intense brain powers have a choice to accept them or not. Let's recall that when Mevlana first received the instructions to proceed with the dictation, she refused. Then, she was reminded that there was a Covenant. We already know that the world's problems do not come from any God; They come from all of us. Consequently, we are the ones who must solve them. This lack of understanding leads to chaos and lack of progress in all societies. It is emphasized that people from all backgrounds must be loved and not subjugated or destroyed. Some societies that oppress or destroy women will then be destroyed. Therefore, Allah together with all other Celestial Powers, hope to increase the conscious level of people all over the world, from all religions and from no religion.

The question is: How do we improve our consciousness so that we, as a Whole, are able to think thoughts of love, unity and peace, without bearing a grudge against anybody and end the thought of separation? It is obvious that this cannot be achieved by force.

The thought of Oneness has to be discovered by each individual who is willing to dig deeply into his/her own thought system. As described in the first chapter, Light conveys information which is knowledge. This leads to awareness and then, to consciousness. We have read that information is reflected from a human to a human who accepts the reflection but for that to happen there has to be coordination. In other words, invisible Beings monitor reflections. Although they cannot interfere, they can guide us. We need reflections to advance but we have to have the willpower to overcome them if we become obsessed with our thoughts to the point of creating chaos. Only our guides and our willpower can help us. However, there is a catch! At this stage, prayers are also necessary, although it is written that religious obsessions are especially dangerous. This may happen when we keep insisting that "My religion is better than yours." Then, we may try and force this idea on people. By the same token, we may say: "My politics is more effective than yours." These are just some of the examples that we are confronted with in our lives while in the 3rd Dimension.

Why do we do that? It is written that we may feel so comfortable in that dimension (meaning with those thoughts) that we become hypnotized and we may become "pawns" to that dimension. That means that other humans, with the same thoughts, manipulate us and use us to commit the chaos in the world. This may lead us to behave in a way that we are not conscious. In other words, our narrowmindedness intensifies to the point that instead of becoming genuine humans, we behave like brutes.

The aim of *The KB* is to guide us to come out of any condition that prevents us from becoming genuine humans. For that reason, the West has a great task. It is expected that all of us, from all backgrounds including women, will march in front.

Then we can all become authentic human beings.

As we have read, this is exactly the meaning of Islam, which may come as a surprise to the Muslim community. Our True-Loving God has planted His seed in us. He exists within us. This is our inheritance. Of course, we are not God. But we have the great potential to create Universes of Thought.

One day, our development will be such that even the way we interpret Thought, will be modified.

It is written that Thought is such an unknown energy, that even the Celestial Beings are not able to define it.

## CHAPTER 35
### WOUNDED WARRIOR:
### WAKE UP AND CHEER

*The Knowledge Book* is not an indoctrination into any faith but a cohesive explanation of humanity in today's times. Therefore, it is a complement to all societies. It can serve to facilitate insights that lead to self-fulfillment and stimulate the thought system. It must be read directly and sequentially from the original in a quiet environment, with love and patience. Prerequisite to the reading, our preconceived ideas as well as fears, need to have been placed aside. After reading, preferably one fascicle per week, for one year, without skipping pages, the reader will notice a big difference in himself/herself. However, he/she must not expect to understand most of it, at least during the first readings. That our learning proceeds slowly and in accordance with our needs should not be considered a problem.

We know that this is the age of Truthfulness, which is very hard to accept by most of us, humans, at this stage in our history. This is because we've allowed the ego to take charge of our lives. For this reason, many people from all walks of life will not like what is written, including some who consider themselves religious or spiritual. If you do not believe that all the developments described, have been planned for centuries and, are now in effect on this planet, just look at the world as it was in pasts centuries, and as it is now in the 21st century.

Do you question the fact that children are now born with pre-knowledge of technology, to the point of using a computer like a pro?

Do you ever question why multitudes are moving from one area to another?

Do you question why "time" appears to have accelerated, and that humans are facing humans like never before in history?

Do you ever question why there are so many natural disasters occurring?

No government can interfere with the events that have been predesigned to contribute to our progress. Furthermore, whether we believe it or not, all events are Divine.

It is understood by the Invisible Forces that we no longer pay much attention to history. Therefore, our sexual revolution which started in the 1960s was implemented to help us remember that we are all descendants of prehistoric beings. It should come as no surprise that we wonder so much about our sexuality. The phallic symbol is present in everyone's mind. It is actually understood that, like a phallus within a vagina, even universes are, creatively, one inside the other. The fact that new physics has accepted the concept that there is no separation, troubles many individuals, even scientists. Our present state of nudity, manifested in the way we are dressing, is also a form of "remembrance." All of us were born naked, and following Adam and Eve, we were probably naked for centuries before we discovered that leaves could conceal our inherent nakedness. Our state of nakedness also serves symbolically to remind us that we are born pure therefore, our connection with the Divine is always primary. However, if we have this awareness, it generally will not last long because the opposite is also implanted in us.

As we go through our ordeals on earth, we may catch glimpses of the state of unity yet, we still cannot avoid facing the opposites, because the system is set up this way, at least for now. It is also written that the fact that there are no trees in the desert is a stimulus to the inhabitants of that area and its surroundings to change their negative thoughts to Love so that they bring positive energies to the area. We all know that trees attract electricity. Some of us may even have known people killed by lightening while sitting or walking near trees. Physicists, scientists, researchers have concluded that trees are the only living substance and, as such, their energy can have an influence in our bodies, it can improve our health. Have you hugged a tree today?

We already know that trees bring positive thoughts to the earth and, therefore they consume negativity. The planting of trees must start with children. They must be instructed to plant trees, especially in areas where they can grow. They must also be encouraged to nurture and love animals and certainly to respect and love all human beings, the ones the parents like and the ones they dislike. Children are the future of our planet and, as such, are born already prepared for events and challenges that we do not yet know about. Parents must never present a false face or lie to their children. Sometimes, we may consider children (and even adults) normal or abnormal. The question is? What is normal these days? What we may consider normal is constantly changing, so that society adapts to new thought-forms for the benefit of mankind, even if we dislike them. In the final analysis, what this means is that we are not teaching anything new, but rather pulling out strings of information we have accumulated in our brain cells. Perhaps the greatest of all missions assigned to us is what has been happening is the past few years, which has been very well planned and orchestrated, and will continue for some time. Indeed, a new stage has been set up so fast and, so unexpectedly, that we are all left shaking in our boots. With thousands, even millions of people moving from continent to continent, this is a chance for humans to face their fellow humans as never before in history. Here is our opportunity to see others as mirrors of ourselves in images of the good, the bad, the ugly and, even the terrifying!

> "All the world's a stage
> And all the men and
> women merely players."
> *As You Like It*
> William Shakespeare

Perhaps now more than ever, we have a chance to see others as our friends, or as enemies. How long the West and the East will play this game is our choice. In any case, we have been set up to go through a new stage in human history, all programmed far in advance and leading to our development for the benefit of mankind.

Recently, our solar system has been producing many storms. Chaos and mental health problems, like depressions increase, all in preparation for happier days.

These happier times will be achieved, peacefully, by the choice of each individual; otherwise, brainwashing could impose a passive state on individuals, resulting in human robots, invented and directed by men. In the system, if we decide to really wash our brains, we have to do it ourselves, in a peaceful manner and, by taking responsibility for our actions and our thoughts. We have to accept the fact that we are guided by Forces that are Invisible and Powerful. We may call those forces, Jesus, God, Allah, Moses, Buddha, or whichever name is in accordance with what we believe. As already mentioned, *The KB* explains that we are biological robots. We are guided by the Divine and created by the Creator, in collaboration with each of us. It is not men that guides us. We are computers of flesh and bones, always renewing ourselves as we keep discovering our Essence. We have mind and soul that cannot be measured, neither can spirit. We also have free will and the ability to choose which path to take. Above all, we have consciousness----a way to understand and even to become.

Again, let's recall what is mentioned in the 1st chapter, that information comes from Light and is knowledge leading to consciousness. Without knowledge there can be no consciousness.

Whereas, the robots created by humans, are also manipulated by humans: They have no free will. We must remember the importance of what we cannot see and feel it inside ourselves. It is about time to start opening up to the Invisible Forces without fear, in order to accept their guidance with joy, love and appreciation.

We know that we have more power than the Invisible Beings. Besides, as already mentioned we, humans, were the first ones to reach God. Even Allah admits this Truth. Consequently, he leaves us, when we are ready, so that we enter the Real and Ultimate world of The Creator of All Creations, while his mission takes him to other worlds. Again, we must appreciate his truthfulness and devotion to his mission. It is true that the Invisible Forces (including Allah) have the power to destroy us at the touch of a button if we are not able to unify our consciousness. However, most religious books tell us that those who are sufficiently advanced in spiritual matters will be transported peacefully to other planets if any force tries to destroy us. This does not mean that we should not cherish our planet, and our mission. It means that we may kill men, but we cannot destroy thoughts. Allah knows that we, like him, are reflections of an energy unknown to us: we are representatives of a Reality that is beyond our comprehension. He knows we are going through the nightmare of separation. In charge of a system that is his last hope, Allah helps us face the reality of who we are, and shows us the way out of the box we are trapped in. We are the ones who blindly grope for a power outside of ourselves when it already abides within us. We received a profound wound in our hearts when we fell asleep and suffered the traumatic experience of a dream of separation. For this reason, we are wounded warriors who have been fighting an invisible Power within ourselves.

A Cosmic Journey to the Unknown is not easy---it is fascinating!

Wounded Warrior, you know you are a sleeping giant: Wake up and cheer.

When we wake up, we'll not only rule ourselves but also save ourselves, our planet and much more.
Let's have faith and love God, whatever concept we have of Him.
We must also love humanity and in spite of it all, never forget that True-Love is always the answer.

***Odete, New York, 2019***

# BIBLIOGRAPHY

*A Course in Miracles*. Copyright © 1975, Foundation for Inner Peace, Inc.

Barnett, Lincoln. *The Universe and Dr. Einstein*. New York: William Sloan Associates Publishers. Revised Edition 1950.

Bigote, Odete M. *You Can Remember Love: Contemplations on Science and Spirituality*. First Books Library, 2000.

Bigote, Odete M. *Before the World Began. The Point of the Encounter of Love and Science*. Tate Publishing and Enterprises, LLC. Oklahoma 2012.

Bohm, David. *Wholeness and the Implicate Order*. London and New York: Routledge & Kegan Paul Ltd., and Methuen, Inc., 1980.

Dunya Kardeslik Birligi Mevlana Yuce Vakfi.
Published: *The Knowledge Book*. Copyright © 1996 Istanbul/Turkiye

Gamow, George. *One, Two, Three Infinity*. Viking, NY. 1961.

Hawking, Stephen W. A *Brief History of Time*. From the Big Bang to Black Holes. New York: Bantam,1988.

Hawking, Stephen W. and Leonard Mlodinow. The Grand Design. Bantam 2010.

Heisenberg, Werner. Physics and Philosophy. The Revolution in Modern Science. Harper and Row, Publishers, Inc. First Harper Torchbook edition published 1962.

Jeans, Sir James. *The Mysterious Universe*. New York: The MacMillan Company,1932.

Paramahansa, Yogananda. *Autobiography of a Yogi*. 1st published in 1946 by the Philosophical Library.

Plato, Laws of. University of Chicago Press, Chicago,1988.

Russell, Bertrand. The Conquest of Happiness. Liveright Publications, New York 1930.

Spalding, Baird T. *Life and* Teaching *of the Masters of the Far East*. Devorss & Co Ca, 1986.

## ABOUT THE AUTHOR

Odete Martins Bigote was born in Lisbon, Portugal and educated in England, Switzerland and the United States. Her background includes the arts, languages, literature, holistic health, yoga instruction, and other spiritual disciplines. She is a lecturer and workshop leader and the author of the following books: You Can Remember Love: Contemplations on Science and Spirituality, and Before the World Began the Point of the Encounter of Love and Science. Odete has written many articles on spirituality and metaphysics, which are published on her website. She produced her own cable TV show for decades and makes her home in New York City.


Please visit her website:
www.odetebigotebooks.com

www.ingramcontent.com/pod-product-compliance
Lightning Source LLC
Chambersburg PA
CBHW071308110426
42743CB00042B/1220